RAW LAW:

A Hip-Hop Guide To Criminal Justice

Muhammad Ibn Bashir, Esq.

RAW LAW

For information about permission to reproduce selections from this book, contact:
The Vandy Publishing Company
112 Oak Street
Newark, NJ 07106
(800) 352-3864

Printed in the United States by Morris Publishing, Kearney, NE

FIRST EDITION: August 2004

Library of Congress Control Number: 2004103342

ISBN: 0-9752744-0-6

Cover Illustration & Graphics:
Donald Wooten of Holla Graphics

Book Layout: Liz Pagan

Lyrics by: E-Blade

Website design: Richard Warr of Initialdesign, Inc.

Information was retrieved from files to illustrate and emphasize points of law and relevant fact patterns. Names of clients have been altered or eliminated to ensure privacy and/or attorney/client privilege.

For further information log onto www.RAWLAW.net

TABLE OF CONTENTS

ACKNOWLEDGMENTS

I never thought that this page mattered until I began to write and reflect. So let me say special thanks to: Yahya and Khadijah Bashir, where you could always go for a prayer, a good debate and a reality check; Hassen Ibn Abdellah, Esq., my brother and "the Amir." Thaki Ismael, Esq., and especially Daryl L. Avery, Esq., who shared his food and his family since '75; Steven J. Brister, Esq., who always offered the best of brotherhood in law school, at his mom's (hi mom) and at the office; the Foxhunters, wherever they may be, for giving me the mike (the next book is about you); Frank Trocino, Esq., Honorable Alison Brown-Jones, JMC, and Honorable Rudolph Hawkins, JSC, for being there; Honorable Walter R. Barisonek for being worthy of respect; the Barrister Law Group of Bridgeport, Connecticut; HOWARD UNIVERSITY and Ubiquity the Family; Professors Samuel Yette and Wallace Terry, journalism professors who both recommended law school and taught social advocacy; Allen D. Lester, Regan and Ernest Montgomery, Janice and Leon Harvey, A'isha Abdul-Aleem, Torian and Tamika Conner, Walter and Monterey (Mona Rae) Stewart, Tasheemah Munda Sessoms, and Claudette Meyers, for having their hearts and doors open; the Warr Family for friendship; Lloyd and Uncle Bobby Stewart, Fatima and Ali Bashir, for paying bills that I could not; Fred Van Doren, Vicky Nia Tankard, Hajj Hesham Jaaber, for encouraging me to write from the heart; Milton "Skip" Waddell, Esq., who told me to sit my "a--" down and take the bar; Donald Wooten of Holla-Graphics, an artist and visionary; my niece Sakina Bashir and Omarr "Uncle O" Bashir for their edits and for helping me understand the language of Hip-Hop; Illiyas Muhammad (E-Blade) your beats and lyrics inspire; AbdurRaheem Muhammad, the day the cop in Prince George's County Maryland killed you is the day I began to write and fight back; MBASH 7, which includes Amirah, Nurideen, and Imani Bashir—my proofreaders, study partners and fan club; Muhammad Na'im Bashir, the most courageous kid I've ever met; Sadiyah Bashir, for helping me remember, FAM-A-LEE. Aliyah, because I always acknowledge beauty and intelligence; and finally, mom, Sakina Bashir, rest in peace and thank you for dreaming for me.

DEDICATION

Dear Aliyah,

This book is dedicated to you. There are many reasons why, and when you read this, you will know why. Remember when we first began to talk and I told you I wasn't sure if I wanted to go to law school? You told me that I had to and that I couldn't or wouldn't be satisfied with not completing my dream (my mother's dream). I listened, and you were right.

You have been so right, so often that I smile at the thought that you're still in my corner. Remember when you said that I should take the DC bar instead of New Jersey, and I didn't listen? I had my own plan on how things would play out. I thought about all the reasons that I gave you for my returning to New Jersey; to save the community, the law firm me and my friends would set up that was going to be "the bomb." Foolish me. You stuck with me, but again, you were right.

I thought back to the many nights that I fell asleep at the table and you covered me. The many times that I couldn't make it here or there, but you covered for me. Remember, when I was invited to be a part of the World Trade Center defense team, you said, NO!? I didn't listen. I learned so much about the law and myself from that experience. Working with Hassen and Bahir was tremendous and I will always be grateful, but again, you were right. That was not the place for me at that time.

You were right when you believed that Maryland was a better place for a family, when you expressed that the profession was causing me health problems. When you suggested that I find another line of work that would allow me to "save souls" without so much stress. You were right.

But I didn't listen... That is until I began to listen to myself as I wrote this book. No more lectures, no more frustration, no more leav-

ing you to fend for yourself while I save the world. I'm listening, I'm hearing.

I'm dedicating this book and myself to doing the thing that I enjoy most in the world and the thing that I do best; smile back at you when you smile at me. I started this journey with you in mind and I think of nothing but finishing it that way; dedicated to making you smile.

If you read this book and sense that I'm angry, well, you'd be right again. I'm angry at the fact that I put anyone else's time before our time, knowing what I know about this system and how it hates my very presence in it. I'm angry that I allowed this lifestyle to confuse what my real purpose is; the one I told you I would be about when we met; the one I forgot when I got into this game. To stand for something!

The test of whether I stand for something or not is going to be you. I know that now. I love you. Always have. Your smiling got me through 17 years of confusion. Can you please forgive me long enough to get me through 17 more?

I can't promise that I won't try to save the world again, but I will promise that I'll respect your opinion (sometimes)—smile.

P.S. Can I come home now?

FOREWORD

Bismillah ir Rahman ir Raheem

This book is affectionately entitled, "A Hip-Hop Guide To Criminal Justice." The book is part fact, part fiction. The part which is fact is reflective of the stories, the law, and the analysis of the system. The part of the book that is fiction are the names and the meshing of various true stories to help the reader understand the point. I changed names and mixed consistent stories at times because I do not think it is appropriate to divulge clients' real names, nor am I attempting to embarrass anyone I might have come into contact with on the road to understanding.

When I began to practice law, I would often find myself lecturing young men and women about the very topics that I write about herein. I began to believe that I could not continue giving the same lectures over and over and that the world could not be saved one case at a time. I also surmised that the world needed saving, unfortunately, one case at a time. What a dilemma. When I began to lecture and speak about the system, I found that so few of the people who are impacted on by the system understand anything about the system. Further, those of us who think that we know, cannot separate the academic exercise of the law from the reality of the system.

Finally, I observed that the system had no intention of educating or liberating the minds of the people because its very survival depends on an under-informed populace. I looked high and low for a way out of this dilemma but could not find one. Always, however, at the end of a saga or a nightmare was some undereducated, poor, or minority kid who looked and sounded like his life was an NWA video. I wondered, often out loud, if the difference between a conviction for "Shyne" and an acquittal for "P. Diddy" had more to do with how "P. Diddy" was marketed than the facts of the case. "P. Diddy"—rich mogul. "Shyne"—thug. I remembered when Tupac was shot in the elevator and when he was accused and convicted of sexual assault. In his "thugness," he was glorified and I wondered if he was being glorified because he stood for something and I just didn't get it. I wondered, what if he was being glorified for standing for nothing and that the generation was satisfied with images that meant nothing so long as they looked and sounded good. I thought about the Mike Tyson rape trial and that "lawyer" he had. Neither he nor Mike seemed to understand the impact image has in a courtroom or, maybe, neither of them cared. I thought about the hit on Biggie Smalls, Jam Master Jay, and many others and wondered if the generation even had a clue about the destructive images that are being blasted across the world, in their name. I thought about how much more of an impact on the lives of people this generation could have if it would just stand for something that matters.

Frankly, I remember Grand Master Flash, Afrika Bambaata, "B-boys," Hip-Hop on the corner, battling to stay alive and fighting for the hearts and minds of its fans. But it wasn't marketable; it was "street," like me. I thought that it was too coincidental that when it became marketable, so did crack cocaine. So did the rise in street drug violence and so did the proliferation of automatic weapons in the same community.

So I began to write and listen and write some more. The language in the book is a bit unconventional, but so is Hip-Hop. So is crime. So is the criminal justice system. I decided to "talk at you," hopefully, without being preachy. I decided to address the issues the way Hip-Hop came at the world back in the day. Challenging and uncompromising. If anyone reads this book from the Hip-Hop culture and thinks that it is a direct attack, they are right. It is meant to be a light in your eyes and once you get past the first blinding hurt, the light is there to guide you through this "hood." I once was told that in order to reach the people you have to speak their language or at least a language they understand.

I'm not so old that I cannot remember Chuck D and Public Enemy saying "Fight the Power." The fact is, I heard this call long before PE, and I understood it.

Having Chuck scream it out again only allowed me to once again, take it to heart. He was calling on a generation to stand up. So am I. I truly believe that this little adventure in faction will help those who want to hear the "real" stand up. Because this book, if nothing else, is real.

Rules Rule

I am a criminal trial attorney. So that there is no mistake, it's what I do, not who I am. I have been doing this for seventeen years; that is staring down the criminal justice system in an effort to be true to who and what I really am. When I was a child, my mother dreamed that I would become a lawyer. She placed that dream in my mind and in my heart. My father taught me that I was created from the best of nations because we encourage what is right and forbid what is wrong. Each and every time I step into a courtroom on a criminal matter, I think of my mother's dream and my father's admonition. I am ready to wage war because, as quiet as it is kept, criminal justice is war.

In this war, you battle, you strategize, you plan and make moves, you attack and you defend. When I go to war, I've learned to take no prisoners because someone's life literally is always on the line. It doesn't matter if the person I am defending is a mass murderer or someone who just got a speeding ticket. The rule for a criminal lawyer is to protect the client's rights, take the matter seriously, WIN. With each battle, each client, each issue, you become hard; hard to get along with, hard-hearted and in my case, just plain ghetto hard.

Consistently, I represent kids from the "hood" or the "streets" who really think they know something that I don't know about the world. But the truth is that the court is no different than the hood. Simply stated, when you know the rules, you can move through any hood without much of a problem. When you do not know the rules or you choose to ignore them, you get "burnt."

Once, I was investigating a matter in a housing project in

Newark, New Jersey. A group of young black males was checking out every move I made, and my car. I knew, when I went out there that night, that this was supposed to be a high crime area known for vehicle thefts and armed robberies. As a precaution, I made contact with a local drug dealer that I represented in the past to tell him that I was going to be in that neighborhood that evening. Unfortunately, I had to conduct my investigation at night in order to get the full effect of the crime scene and I knew I needed someone, anyone, to "have my back."

When my back was turned, one little punk made a move for my car. I could hear it as the kid took off in my car, leaving me in Newark, with no way home. I was "pissed" off. I was probably helping out his brother or his uncle, maybe even his daddy, but this little sucker didn't care about anything but "boosting my joint" and showing off for his friends. The friends stood laughing as I came running around the corner, just in time to see my ride disappear into the night. For one brief moment, I had forgotten the rules and now I was stranded. I grew up in a housing project just like this one so I should have known better. When reality set in, I saw myself, as I am sure they saw me, suit, tie, wrong neighborhood, late at night; just ripe for a "stick-up kid." I sensed that it wouldn't be long before some other punk with a gun got the nerve to approach me, that is, if I didn't remember where I came from. I walked over to the group of young boys, stared down the one with the biggest laugh and spoke.

"Yo! You, you with the mouth. You know that boy who stole my shit?"

"Man, I don't know what shit you talking about."

Everyone laughed.

"Cool. Keep it funny. I don't know who he is, but I can describe you and when the police get here, you 'wearing' the theft. And in case you think that shit is funny too, this just became a 'jack' with a black 22, that I think you had on you. Scared me half to death! That should hold your little smart ass in case you're a juvenile and think you can walk away from it tonight."

"I ain't do shit," he said angrily.

"Yes, you did dog. You saw your boy ready to steal my car, knew it was wrong and weren't man enough to stop him. Now, it comes down to your word and the word of these little wannabe thugs against mine. So guess who's wearing it?"

"Fuck you man!" he countered.

"By the way, for the rest of you, I'm gonna walk down to the liquor store and call a cop. If I get my shit back, we have no beef. But if I don't, I got a partner named Omar who rolls through here. He's my next call. And I ain't asking him to lock nobody up. I'm asking him to make sure that the next time I come in his neighborhood, the young boys show me some respect."

I turned and walked away. The liquor store was two long blocks away. With each step that I took, I got angrier and angrier. This time however, I followed the rules; walked and looked like I belonged there, and it was working. No stick-up, no threats. I was in the liquor store for approximately 15 minutes when Omar arrived. After all, this was his turf, his hood. In his business, it was important that he check things out. I told him what happened and described the kids involved. He left. Twenty minutes later, a young black male drove up in my car and parked it on the corner. The ignition was popped. He left a screwdriver in the car so that I could start it and get home. Everything that I had in the car, except the ignition, was still in the car. I didn't speak to him and he didn't speak to me. The next night, I was back on the block taking pictures. I parked the car in the same spot (another rule) and the same group of young boys showed up.

"Hey, Bashir."

"Oh, we know each other now? Cool."

"Yo. Like last night. My bad, naameen."

"I'm hearin' you. Come here and make yourself useful. I need you to stand here and point at this sign, so I can photograph it."

"Yo Bashir, let me get in the pictures too."

"Me too."

By the time I finished, all of these kids helped me photograph a crime scene. They explained what they knew about the crime I was investigating and told me some things about the various witnesses that I would be questioning at trial, much of which I used to impeach their credibility. I eventually represented three of the six boys as adults, one for drugs, one for car theft, and one for armed robbery.

I got to know them well over the years. Omar dropped out of college and hit the streets. He had an exceptional business sense that was being wasted and utilized in the drug game. Another of the kids, Shuz, would always show up in court for my trials and discuss strategy with me. He said he always wanted to be a lawyer, but got caught up in the thug life. Eventually, the stick-up kid killed the car thief over a girl that didn't really want either of them and is doing 20 years in prison. And me, I still go in and out of courts and hoods alike, trying to explain the rules of both, each to the other. Unfortunately, neither is listening.

Now, I am just too angry to keep spitting into the wind. Now, I know that the criminal justice system and the hood are both losing propositions. The Prophet Muhammad (peace be upon him) once said, that the best of us in faith is the one who sees injustice and changes it with his own hands. If he cannot change it with his hands, then he speaks out against it. If he cannot speak out against it, he at least despises it in his heart. If I could, I would rip this system apart and start it all over because it is seriously lost. I can't, so I have to speak out.

And since I represent so many of this generation in criminal matters, let me say this loud and clear. The Hip-Hop generation is a fraud. A farce. It's a generation of multi-million dollar stars with little to no positive impact on the "hood" that carries their jocks. It's a generation of images that make you fiend for the flavor, but also attacks your core of values. It's a generation of brilliance, with no one having a sense or an ounce of education. It's a generation of computers and videos and no sense of history and context.

This is why it is supposedly "cool" to be "hard" when you have never faced a hard day in your life. While others find it's so "hard" to be "cool" when they have never gotten a break from their day to day living hell. It's a generation of no rules, even though everyone recognizes that there must be a rule out there somewhere (so long as it doesn't apply to them). A young boy can respect the local drug dealer and disrespect his mother in the same breath. He can kill someone over a pair of sneakers while he demands that he be respected as a man.

I once sat down with the boys and girls from the Newark posse and we discussed the rules of engagement on the streets and in the courts. I walked away from that meeting feeling the same way I have when walking from numerous meetings in various hoods. This generation is confused. The confusion stems from its collective lack of education (or appreciation of education) and the mixed messages being targeted at this generation.

Look! This generation has little girls having babies before they are old enough to sit up straight; girls who confuse the concept of womanhood, which they may be entering, with the concept of motherhood which they are not ready, willing, or able to handle. This generation has 18-year-old boys supporting their grandmothers with the money they make because they "sling rocks" (sell drugs). Grandmas, back in the day, would never tolerate that. So the little rock slinger is now the breadwinner, the man of the house, demanding a level of respect he is not mature enough to handle. Frankly, it doesn't matter to me whether the little breadwinner is a drug dealer or a multi-million dollar athlete or entertainer. He doesn't have enough manhood days in to be a leader or a role model. But his money or celebrity makes him someone important, someone to emulate. Get Real!

Every time I find myself involved in one of these discussions, there is some kid who says, "You just don't understand." But I do understand. I understand that I don't know any old minority drug dealers, which in my profession, tells me that black boys will never live long enough to be gangsters, like the mob.

I understand that guns in the minority communities are making someone not of that community, filthy rich, and giving some other "filthy rich" member of that other community, a reason to build a prison in some rural community, where the only minorities in the community, are in the prison. I understand that young people are being taught to be frustrated by the image of overnight success that their contemporaries demonstrate. And I understand, that when you target a community to obey your passions, "your thirst," or to "just do it," you are training that community to act without thinking... a road map to a life of crime. It is really hard out there. But think of this generation and/or yourself as a generation of great swimmers left in an ocean. As you navigate your way through your life, you learn to admire the Kobes, J. Lo's, the Nas's, and the Russell Simmons' of the world.

You marvel at how beautifully they stroke, how fast they swim, because in this water no one is better. Except the sharks. One such shark is the criminal justice system. Some of you will get out of the water safely, and sure, even I "wanna be like Mike." But the sharks own the ocean and the best way to keep from getting chewed up and swallowed, is not to get in. That's the first rule of criminal justice. DO NOT GET IN.

The second rule is, when you stroll into this hood, come correct. That means if you have a lawyer get him/her on your case immediately. If you cannot afford to pay a lawyer, get in touch with the public defender immediately. Finally, rule number three is simple. Learn who is on your side and who your enemy is. In most criminal cases, the enemy is clear. It is the system itself (that sometimes means the judge, the prosecutor, your lawyer, and the rules). In order to teach you this, I have opened my files. The stories you will read are real. I have borrowed facts where I needed to and changed some in order for you to learn where the system is coming from and where it is headed. Just understand that this system has never been anywhere you wanted it to be and is not headed anywhere you want it to go.

Public Pretenders

I laugh inside each and every time I hear someone say that this is the best system known to man. I always think that man must lack common sense if he cannot come up with something significantly better than this nonsense. My advice is to avoid this monster if you can, for as long as you can. It is called criminal justice. Often, you find the criminal, they come on all sides of the system. Seldom, do you find any justice.

The process begins with an accusation and/or the commission of a crime. This, on many occasions, leads to the arrest of a person. That arrest is generally done by police officers. Fortunately or unfortunately, depending on your vantage point, police officers are human. They bring to the job every prejudice and every stereotype that most of society has regarding so-called criminal conduct. No matter how good a person this cop is, he or she has a job that, for the most part, is to maintain order, maintain the status quo. He works in a job where he is not respected and the job itself is less service than it is community care-taking. Often, he is doing his "job" and is detached from the community he "protects and serves." He does not live there. He has no real vested interest in the success or failure of the community. He is just doing his "job." The businessman isn't much different in his eyes from the drug dealer. The elderly are not much different from the young. The community knows him by name, by car, and by reputation, but all he knows is a select number of families because he has arrested daddy in the past. This of course is not true in all communities. White communities just do not seem to have this problem.

Routinely, the police are the ones making or breaking many of the cases that come to court. Their veracity is always an issue. They therefore receive training on how to recognize criminal activity, how to write proper reports, how to testify, and how to make a presentation in court. They research the case law to stay on top of the constitutional issues. This training and experience is often what makes them believable when they come to court. It is also the reason why they lie so well, violate the citizen's rights so easily. It's why you have corrupt cops, even criminal cops in Miami, Los Angeles, Newark, Baltimore, Detroit, New York, Philadelphia, New Orleans; pick a city. But even when they are not corrupt, they are, at the very least very well trained.

The concept of **Driving While Black (DWB)**, that is stopping black or Latin motorists on a pretext and searching their vehicle for illegal contraband, is a concept that arises from the fact that officers are trained to see blacks and Latinos as potential criminals. With that training and experience, they now design a way around the law that will allow them to manipulate the motorist, as well as the **Fourth Amendment**. This has gone on for years and is just now gaining public scrutiny. The point is that the person who does this kind of blatant violation of civil and constitutional rights and humiliates and disrespects a black motorist is, if not criminal minded himself, often a "decent guy," just doing the job he was trained to do. So is the cop who is just stopping and patting down black and Latino males, in violation of their rights, because they are hanging out on the corner. I just wonder how many black men have criminal records, cannot vote, or serve on juries, be a full participant in their citizenship because some state trooper or some "narco" was just doing the job the way he was trained to do it. Someone out there is calling this justice while others say it is just power doing what power does.

Often, cases are brought to the court because of "**lay witnesses**." These are normal citizens who either observe or hear something related to the crime and have the courage to come forward. Seldom in the court system, do these lay witnesses not have an interest in the outcome. They are often the victim, a friend of the victim, or someone who is just fed up with the crime going on in their neighborhood. Lay witnesses bring one unique aspect to a case—familiarity. Most of the time they know the victim or the accused.

They are perhaps the most credible people in the process when they have no interest in the outcome. Yet, they are subject to all the rules of manipulation that the process offers from all sides, all in the name of seeking out truth.

When they testify for the State, and they are credible, you, as a defendant, are in trouble. However, the more contact they have with the police and law enforcement, including prosecutors, the less credible they become. Why? Because the police and the prosecutors have an agenda. They want to win. They will take whatever course it takes to win. Often, that course is to let the case speak for itself. Far more often, it is the concept of over-trying a case. They interview the same witness over and over in an effort to get this witness prepared for trial thereby opening the door to multiple statements from the witness, inconsistencies, and the very serious charge of coaching. Coaching means that the government has a theory of the case and is constantly feeding that theory to the witness. The witness is thereafter adopting the government's version or just agreeing because the government says this is what happened. If a "lay person" really saw or perceived an event, you don't have to tell him/her what he/she saw. But prosecutors and/or investigators, seeking convictions at the expense of justice, do. When that happens, and it happens more than you will ever believe, your lay person loses credibility, and rightly so.

Don't be fooled. Many of these lay witnesses are the "drug kingpin" who made a deal to rat out his "posse" and any other innocent party they think they may have a beef with. Sometimes, they turn on the competition and, far too often, they lie on someone who they think got them in trouble. They are listed as the "CI" (**Confidential Informant**—anonymous tip) but, they are usually the criminal minded just working time off their own bid at your expense. They are the disgruntled ex-girlfriend, the jilted ex-boyfriend, or some "hero" trying to feel important at the expense of the truth.

The public servant who will decide whether the alleged facts amount to a crime is the **Prosecutor**. These legal eagles initially have the obligation of determining whether or not there are facts that should be prosecuted. Eight out of ten times, these public servants accept what a police officer says as if the officer has the integrity of Jesus. They begin their service by presenting the matters to the **Grand Jury**. The Grand Jury is a group of citizens convened to hear the government's evidence or to investigate a matter being presented by the government. No person can or should be held over to stand trial on a matter that could send them to prison unless and until they are indicted by the Grand Jury. Frankly, this demand, which comes from the **Fifth Amendment to the United States Constitution**, is so absurd that it borders on lunacy. You have all heard the expression that a "prosecutor could indict a ham sandwich if he wanted to." Nothing in the criminal justice system can be truer. It simply means that in the Grand Jury, the government has all the control and power. If they want you indicted, you are getting indicted.

In the Grand Jury, you have a majority rule vote. Customarily, twenty-three persons are impaneled and evidence is presented to them. If twelve agree, the defendant is **indicted**. If less than twelve, the defendant is **no billed** (not indicted). The difference in whether a defendant is indicted or not, is basically up to the prosecutor. There is no defense attorney present. There is no cross-examination. In some jurisdictions, you have the right to a **probable cause hearing**, but much of what is determined at these hearings may never get before a Grand Jury. If there is **exculpatory evidence** (evidence suggesting your innocence) the prosecutor seeking to indict, controls how and when it is presented to the point where most Grand Juries simply follow the lead of the prosecutor.

Eventually, you get to court and some judge tells a **petit jury** (the ones who decide if you are guilty or not guilty) that the fact that you have been indicted means nothing. It is just a way of bringing the matter to the court. Think about what you thought of whenever you heard someone was indicted. You did not think, "Oh, he's innocent. I can't wait for his real trial." You thought, like most people do, "I wonder what he did?" An indictment means something even if only subliminally.

Most of these public servants are relatively fair-minded people. They, unfortunately for the defendant, work in a position that gives them power over people's lives and they are taught to use the full force of that power. The one thing they possess that they do not use enough of, is discretion. Far too many cases are prosecuted or go to trial that should not because the prosecutor claims they have no discretion or are unwilling to exercise it. As a defendant, you are hoping that your lawyer can convince the prosecutor to cut you a break, use his discretion to prosecute or not to prosecute. But far too often, the discussion goes something like this:

"Look, we have a kid with no prior criminal involvement and you're offering him prison? This case can go away if you offer him a plea that comes with probation."

"But eluding (attempting to escape the police by use of a vehicle and creating a substantial risk of injury to another) is a second degree offense. He's facing a maximum of 10 years."

"So he's charged with a second degree offense. You have the discretion to amend it to a third degree offense and offer him probation and it's over. You have no injuries, no damage to the vehicle, and the reports say it happened at 2 a.m., so no one would have been out there to be threatened."

"I'll offer him a plea to second degree; treat it as a third degree for sentencing. The recommendation is five years in prison. That'll be the judge's call."

"You're kidding right? He can get that if he took the matter to trial and lost."

I often wonder what it must be like for a prosecutor who finally realizes that the officers that make or break their cases everyday, make up the rules on the street as they go along. Once, a prosecutor asked me if I dislike all cops. I have never expressed a personal dislike for any cop, but have expressed a dislike for the way most of them who wind up in court (I said most) do their jobs. I often ask these public pretenders to take a walk with me through the hood, not as a prosecutor, but as a citizen. What they will see is the anger on the faces of young black males when the police are around. They will see the mutual disrespect that the police and the community have for each other. They will see how quickly a mind can be changed by something positive said or done, and how quickly a mind can be shaped by the negatives. I grew up thinking that eventually every so-called black male in the community would be either in prison or dead by the time he was 21. Not many males from my generation escaped that prophecy. The world saw us differently and we saw the world differently. Unfortunately, most prosecutors cannot grasp that there is a world out there that functions totally in juxtaposition to all they know and all they have ever seen. So they trudge on with blinders. They exercise the discretion in the job the way they do because they cannot identify with what goes on in the real world. If they did, they would check these cops and lying lay witnesses at the door.

At the end of the day, when they finish practicing law on the backs of far too many people who do not deserve the kind of outcome they receive, they go to their homes thinking they did "justice." They have protected the way things are and the way they will stay until someone shows the courage it takes to change this. The next time you hear a prosecutor stand up and say, "Good morning, my name is X, and I represent the State," understand that they are saying, "I represent the status quo" and are only pretending to represent the people.

Every person who is charged with a criminal offense is entitled to be represented by a lawyer. This rule comes to you courtesy of the **Sixth Amendment to the United States Constitution**. If you cannot afford an attorney, one will be appointed for you. In most jurisdictions, this person is called the **Public Defender** (PD). He or she works for the various states or are under contract by the government and is assigned to represent indigent defendants. Since most of the persons charged with criminal conduct cannot afford an attorney, the public defender is his only hope.

Often, some of the best work you will ever see will come from the public defender. Often, some of the worst as well. Public defenders are knee deep in the battle everyday. They work hand in hand with the same prosecutor and judge for lengthy periods of time and develop the type of quid pro quo relationship that often should lead to the best deals and plea bargains. They try quite a few cases during the course of a particular term and are seasoned and often trial tested. What else can you ask for from a lawyer? A little personal attention and integrity would be a start. At times, this job can be so overwhelming. Some days they see anywhere from five to forty-five people all wanting the same personal attention and all deserving the same personal attention. Unfortunately, the same advantage that they have in court is also their nemesis as a public defender. The judge wants them to dispose of all of their matters quickly. The PD knows it is impossible, but he tries because he wants to keep that cordial relationship that benefits the majority of the clients. So when someone's mother asks about her son who is represented by the public defender, the PD appears aloof, disinterested and rude. Getting the plea done is more important at this moment than the "story" the defendant or his mother is telling. Since the public defender is the only representation these defendants can afford, they take their "lawyer's" advice and plead guilty not ever knowing that the PD never even read the file. Their reputation is that of the ultimate Public Pretender. It's a reputation that they do not deserve, but it is one that is earned through a lot of hours of trying to serve more than one master.

Compared to their counterparts (the prosecutor) these public servants are a little closer to the real world. They see innocent persons go to jail and guilty persons walk everyday. They have neither the resources nor the manpower to compete with the government, but they fight on. The problem with them is that they are the only game in town and often their decisions or lack of decisions impact on the entire process.

"I only met with the public defender for 10 minutes and all we talked about was me pleading guilty, and I ain't do shit."

"I can't get in touch with my public defender and trial is next week."

"I don't know who my lawyer is, last month I had a different public defender."

"This public defender is selling me out."

"I need to get me a real lawyer."

"They say they want to help, but they sound like the prosecutor."

—Real sentiments from real people looking for help from the only resource they have.

It's the second toughest job in town (behind police work) but somebody's got to do it. The job begins at 8 a.m. and ends at 5 p.m., and no one pretends that they want to serve the public after hours.

In order to attract lawyers from the private sector, the public defender's office will frequently offer to pay the private lawyer to take on some of their cases. Most private criminal lawyers will tell you that they charge an hourly rate for out of court time, a substantially higher rate for in-court time; bill for calls, copying, investigators, and office visits (just for starters). They will probably charge a flat fee as a retainer, as well. The public defender may pay private attorneys only $25 to $75 per hour. What a private attorney may charge to represent you in a criminal matter may be nearly ten times more than what he or she will get from the public defender to handle your case. Therefore, there is no real incentive for the private lawyer to take your case from the PD. Fortunately, this system is one based on exposure. The more a lawyer is seen in court, the more likely he or she will pick up clients, and cash. Many private lawyers sign on to the public defender list for just that reason. The PD will consistently provide them with clients while they establish themselves (learn) and make a little cash on the side. These are the guys practicing law when you really need someone who "ain't practicing," someone ready for the real game.

So you hire a private attorney. Many of the private attorneys say that they want to help and want to be in the forefront of the fight to establish some semblance of justice in the system. They are lying. They want to get paid. If the client has some money or maybe an appealing issue that may get them on Court TV, they will be in your corner. If not, you unfortunately become another fee who spends too much time with collect calls and much too much time asking the same question about the law. After all, it's only your one life on the line while we have any number of lives we have to collect fees from.

You hired this attorney because of his reputation or his name (many times it's because of his race) having never checked him out to see if he has any "skills." He or she is cool in the beginning, promising you the world. "You can beat that." "Sure with no priors, we can get you probation." When they have as much of your loot as they feel they can get, they flip. "Look, I'm tired of coming back here, the deal is what it is, take it or leave it." "You really don't want to take this to trial. You can't win." "By the way, doesn't your mother owe me some money?"

You have fallen for all the usual manipulation and lies from someone trained to manipulate and lie, and now find yourself on a collision course with prison asking your lawyer, "What happened?"

It's about money and if you have real money, you can seek out the justice they tell you exists. If you have an education, you can understand the real from the pretense. If you have both, you probably will not find yourself in the system or if you do make the big time, you have the clear advantage. Right, "P. Diddy?"

The **Judge** and **Jury** are also interested players in this search for justice. Judges are often those public servants called on to lecture the country about the greatness of the system. They give great lectures, but little else. They tell you that the jury system and a trial by jury are the best ways to vindicate defendants and to assure the state is protected. As a defendant, you could and should care less about protecting the state and you do not want a jury trial. In fact, all you really want, if you are innocent, is for someone to recognize your innocence. A trial is just the path that you reluctantly travel in search of that recognition. (If you are guilty, all you are really looking for is for the government to make you an offer you cannot refuse). On that path, you are looking for a judge or jurors who can and will be fair and impartial. The system says it wants that also. In order to determine who can be fair and impartial, the jurors are asked voir dire questions (preliminary questions about their background). Often, these questions tend to do nothing more than to eliminate minority jurors or jurors with the same or similar background of the defendant (you know, a jury of his peers).

"Have you ever been a victim of a crime?"

"Have you or anyone you have known ever been accused or convicted of a crime?"

"Can you judge the testimony of a police officer the same as any other person?"

It's a known fact that crime disproportionately impacts on poor/minority communities. It is also a known fact that policing is more aggressive in minority communities. It is clearly more likely for a minority person to have been accused, convicted, or related to someone who has been accused or convicted of a crime. Many people of color answer these questions and immediately subject themselves to a challenge by the prosecution. Once the prosecutor hears that you, as a minority, have been accused or that a relative has been accused, they will almost always kick you to the curb. As I watch and listen to the various questions, I am dumbstruck by how few white and/or affluent citizens have the same or similar responses to these questions. When they do, they tell you about being a victim of burglary or about "Junior" who was in drug rehab, but is now doing fine.

Contact with the police is universally judged as being a negative for a minority juror and a positive for a white juror. Yes, the system says it wants people who can be fair, but the make up of the jury panels usually reflects who the system thinks is worthy of being called fair. As a defendant, you sit there and watch and think, "This isn't fair at all." By the time you recognize it, it's too late; you're in it.

Now, you know most of the players in this drama called criminal justice. The only player missing is you. This book is all about you. It's about rules and decision-making and it's a warning for whoever is out there willing to listen. The rules will and should help you understand that this is no place to be. It is a game that is played on a life and death level because crime is played on that level. In the 21st century, the game is changing. It never respected you as an accused or as a person and it is now in full sprint, attacking every liberty or right you think that you have. It's now about secret evidence, profiling, media manipulation, science, fear, race, money, and abuse of power. It is a game of images and stereotypes; myths and pretense. For the most part, these things have nothing to do with the ultimate goal, which is the search for the truth. I have found that in this system there are only two truths. If you get caught in the system by accident, mistake, or subterfuge, there can be no justice no matter how the case is resolved. However, if you choose a path that leads you into this system knowing that everything in it is designed to work against you, and knowing that everyone in the system despises you and disrespects your position, you may get exactly what you deserve. That may be the only justice there is.

"So if you don't know, now you know."

CDS: A Desperate Game, for Desperate People

He's about 5'6" to 6' tall. Pants two sizes too big. Of course, he's black. You know him or you know of him. He's your brother, your boyfriend, your cousin, or maybe your best friend. He's smart. He could probably be a lawyer or a doctor if he ever got his head on straight or maybe got a break. But like so many wrongheaded young men, he thinks that what you have makes you a man; who you know makes you important. He's WRONG, but who's going to tell him?

Anyhow, at this point, it doesn't really matter. His name is Antoine, Raheem, June Bug, or Smooth, depending on whom you ask. If you ask him about life, he hesitates, thinks, and replies... "You do what you gotta do to survive." This sentiment is the philosophy of the desperate and as an attorney representing persons charged with criminal offenses, I have the unenviable task of being role model, counselor, lawyer, employee, and confidant, to the desperate.

It's February of any year and it's a little past 10 p.m. Antoine is standing on the corner talking to some friends. A police unit rides up slowly. Someone spots it and yells "Five O" or "88" or "One Time." (All street expressions of police presence). Everyone turns to look and then begins to walk away. What is about to happen is a process that has put thousands of Antoines in jails and prisons across this country. Someone discards an item. The police see the item. They exit their vehicle, search the ground and find the item. They decide to check the contents and it appears to be crack cocaine. Twenty-one vials. Antoine is arrested.

This scenario is one that occurs daily on the streets of America's inner cities and is becoming more prevalent each day in suburban neighborhoods. Is Antoine a criminal? Is he guilty of possession of the drugs? Well, the narcotics were NOT Antoine's, but he's about to get "played" in a way he never contemplated.

For the purposes of the criminal justice system, Antoine has been arrested and charged with the offense, (probably) **possession of CDS (Controlled Dangerous Substances)** and **possession with the intent to distribute CDS**. Whether they were his drugs or not will not matter to anyone other than him and maybe his mother who cannot believe that her son has been arrested. Often, mom is willing to stick with her baby to the bitter end. Dad, sorry, I don't see enough of them in this scenario to comment on their thinking. Not even Antoine's lawyer believes what he says. The lawyer is often a public defender who is far too busy to give the matter the serious look that Antoine wants him to give. He's heard this story before, far too many times to personally connect with Antoine and, after all, the "deal" (plea bargain) being offered by the State is a good one. Antoine's only hope, which usually is a desperate one, is that the person who dropped the drugs comes forward and admits that they were his AND that the officer who arrested him will admit that he did not see who dropped the items.

How likely is this? Consider that the person who dropped the items did so because he did not want to get arrested. Unless he is a very good friend (most drug dealers are not) he's thinking, "Antoine can beat that without my help; after all it wasn't his stuff." It's not that they (drug dealers) never come forward. But even if they do, I've seen an aggressive prosecutor charge both he and Antoine and let them fight it out in court. Also, consider that in order for the officer to arrest Antoine, he has to have a reasonable belief that a crime was committed and that the arrested person is the one who committed the crime. In the law, this concept is called **probable cause**. How likely is it that he will arrest Antoine and then admit that he arrested the wrong guy? Again, happens, but not very often.

As the police are putting the handcuffs on Antoine, he knows that he hates that feeling. He is scared, but he puts on a front because his "peeples" are watching. If you are one of his "peeps," don't just stand there—call his mother, father, or someone. He needs help! Was Antoine a victim? You all have heard the expression, "in the wrong place at the wrong time." Your own neighborhood generally is that wrong place. This sounds ridiculous, horrifying, crazy, but the reality is that your neighborhood is under attack from ALL sides. Drug dealers in your neighborhood mean you and the "hood" no good. They profit from people's misery, vices, and weaknesses, oftentimes arguing that they are just "trying to get paid." Many young boys enter this lifestyle in order to have some pocket money, to fit in, and/or to have some fun. Often, the money and the lifestyle attract competitors.

The natural consequences are robberies, the perceived need for protection, guns, and violence. Eventually, they find that they're in a "game" that is played at a life and death level. Those who resist the excitement and its temporary high survive. Those who don't see a future in something else, settle for this lifestyle with the ultimate outcome being jail and death. The lifestyle is as addictive as the drugs themselves. Imagine being 16-years-old with little or no opportunity to make it in the NBA or entertainment industry. You go to school everyday and they teach you that the people with money are the "successful." You, on the other hand, are being trained to work like a slave for your entire life and struggle to get bills paid each week. After all, you don't really have lawyers and doctors as mentors in your hood. Then, you "sling a few rocks" one night for your boy and you pocket a "G" in one day of work. Your gear is up overnight. Your stomach is full and you help mom pay the rent for the first time. You like helping mom, hell, she's always been there for you. And the girlies see you differently. You don't really care that they see dollar signs, but you know that if that's all that they see, you can do that too. You're in it. You're hooked. And you, unfortunately don't have enough manhood days in, or manhood dues paid to help you decide that this game is destructive and a set up designed to destroy you and your community.

A former drug dealer once told me, "My girl brought my daughter to the prison to see me. She was one. She had nothing and me being in prison wasn't giving her anything. I promised her that when I got out I would do whatever it took to make sure I didn't leave her out there like that again. I saw my daughter again when she was three and it was like she had grown up and I missed the whole thing. Think about this, my little shorty was 3-years-old before I even was able to hold her... The lifestyle is as addictive as the drugs. When I go around my boys, it's ill. I see the loot, the women, the clothes. It's tempting as hell to get back in the game. I'm glad I have this little girl to keep me straight. Without her, I know I'd be in it again. And probably in prison again."

When his daughter turned 5-years-old, he and his lady decided to get married. The wedding got him in a little debt. His boys said they would pay the debt if he would deliver a little package to Kentucky for them. He knew it was part of the game, but decided it "couldn't hurt." After all, it would only be this one time. The Metro police were waiting for him as he came out of the terminal with two kilos of cocaine in his bag. His daughter will be 17-years-old when he gets out of prison.

The fear drug dealers bring to a community, forces the community to make choices that it does not want to make. Neighbors who don't want their kids associated with trouble are barring up their windows and trying to find any legal way to get to the suburb. No one wants to live in a community where kids with less than a ninth grade education and an even lower level of community pride or self-respect, play war games on the street, to the destruction of innocent babies and grandmothers. They take with them their sense of community and love for the neighborhood and leave behind friends and family who often have no way to stop the spread of crime. The choices for these communities are limited to citizens' action against drugs, which usually means getting out into the streets or seeking more police help. More police in the community to stop drugs means more arrests and inevitably more innocent bystanders arrested. Communities have literally given up their civil liberties in order to be free from drugs and its bad air. Such things, as **racial profiling**, the "**plain view doctrine**," and **exigent circumstance searches** have carved into your right to be free from unreasonable searches or seizures because communities want to be free from drugs.

And since this is supposed to be reality based, let's get real. There are certain communities (black/Latino/poor) where the police generally do not respect the rights of the citizens, and are as much a part of the problem as the street level drug dealer. When it comes to drugs, the police in your hood are always "suspicious," are operating based on stereotypes and profiles and because of this, make far more mistakes than they care to admit. Those who are "good cops" are desperate to solve the problem. You can tell a community that has a police force interested in the people. The cops are out there in the community with programs, talking, relating, and meeting people. They are fighting for the minds of the young and the hearts of the old people. If your community doesn't have any of this on a regular, consistent basis, question their commitment. If that sounds like an accusation, that's because it is!

Then, there are those who are "bad cops." They are lazy and really believe that even the arrest of the wrong person is justified because it sends a message to whoever is "out there" being incorrect. Policing, to this cop, is a "job" in your community, and the only one to be respected, is him. They have these slogans that they operate under like, "We own the night." You know them when you see them roll through your hood. They smirk, pat you down because they can, laugh in your face because they know that if you get arrested for no reason, in court, it comes down to your word against theirs and they don't get prison if they lose, you do. Many even believe that the neighborhoods where street level drug dealing occurs regularly, have nothing in them worthy of protecting. I can make this statement because I have interviewed, examined, cross-examined, and represented the "good" and the "bad" of the police force.

Finally, there is the legislature (the lawmakers) who have passed laws that target minority communities. Drug laws that enhance the penalties for conduct within 1,000 feet of school property or 500 feet of public property, or crack versus powder cocaine, disproportionately impact on minority communities by design. These so-called civil servants know that there is a school, housing project, or public park on almost every corner in the inner-city and the mandatory penalties they propose for these drug crimes are only designed to keep the prison population steady, and satisfy the prison construction, and law enforcement lobbies knowing that their children do not face the same fact scenario, yet. These laws are racist in nature and these lawmakers are turning their collective backs away from anyone who shows that the government is bringing the drugs into the country. All of these actions by government and law enforcement are related to their collective disrespect for people of color and poor people who have historically been considered not worthy of the full participation in America, and as people "jockin," legitimate Americans and their dreams. If you think this sounds similar to statements you have heard or read from organizations like the Klan or Aryan Nation, you are right. The difference is that poor white racists show their disrespect by dragging blacks on the back of a truck, lynching one, or maybe shooting eight or nine minorities before killing themselves. The legislators drag minorities into the criminal justice system and lynch them there. Often, however, legislators have the same disrespect for poor miseducated white racists.

In our first scenario, Antoine is an innocent victim of circumstance. In most jurisdictions, by the time the process has worked itself out, he may have a criminal record. What should he know immediately upon being arrested?

Each and every person in the United States of America has the right to remain silent. This right comes to you by way of the **Fifth Amendment to the United States Constitution**. Under most circumstances, it does you no good at all to talk to the police. At the point of your arrest, you should perceive the police as your worst enemy, although they will almost always tell you they are your friends and that what you say to them can only help you. In the case of **Miranda v. Arizona**, the U.S. Supreme Court made it incumbent upon law enforcement who wishes to question someone, to advise them of their rights. This advice, known as **Miranda warnings**, is to protect you from "**custodial interrogation**"—meaning being questioned by police while in police custody. This surprises many people when it is described in these terms. You have watched all the police and court-room dramas on TV whereby the police always read the person his rights when he's being arrested. Once arrested, the police MAY read you your rights, so that if you say something they can use it.... THAT'S THE ONLY REASON. So when you show up at my office saying, "They didn't read me my rights," I'm only interested in your answer to one question. "Did you talk or give a statement?" If you didn't, it doesn't matter one bit.

After these "rights" are read to you, the police will normally ask you if you understand them. If you do not understand, they cannot question you. If you do understand, you will be asked, on most occasions, if you wish to give up these rights and talk to the police about what happened. You may be given a form to sign saying that you waive your rights. This is used as evidence that you said you understand and wanted to talk. You do not have to sign. Refusing to sign is often interpreted as evidence that you did not give up your rights. Please keep your mouth shut. Nine out of ten times when a suspect talks to the police without an attorney present, the statement is used to convict him. You can't say enough good things about yourself to get released, so shut up! If you decide to speak with the police with an attorney present, his or her job is to protect you. Listen to him/her when they tell you not to answer a certain question, or group of questions, especially, if you're paying them.

But what if Antoine says something before his rights are read to him?

The answer is simple. He's Hit! If there is a way for it to be used against him, it will be.

"I was only out there five minutes." He thinks that helps him. However, five minutes is long enough to establish identification. It also establishes presence at the scene of the crime. Antoine has corroborated most of what the State would have to prove in order to establish his guilt.

How can they use that statement against him, if he says it before he's arrested or before his rights are read to him?

Miranda rights are granted to someone in the custody of the police, which customarily means under arrest. This protection against incriminating yourself does not extend to non-custodial questions or answers. Most smart police officers will let you say whatever you want to before they arrest you and someday you will read it in a police report or hear the officer testify to it. They sometimes start you off by saying, "We just want to talk to you." This approach is intended to get you to open up and when you do, "it's a wrap."

"We have at least three witnesses that place you at the scene with a gun in your hand." The officer, who suggested this to the suspect, did so immediately, before placing him under arrest. Unfortunately, the suspect fell for this bait and responded.

"Who? Those drug dealers? Who's gonna believe them?" In this felony murder trial, the prosecutor argued that this was a statement of motive. She stated that the defendant believed he could rob someone in this neighborhood because the only witnesses would be drug addicts or drug dealers with little to no credibility. GUILTY… life in prison. If you volunteer the information, talk just to hear yourself, count on hearing it again.

Can you be forced to give a statement? Yes and No.

No, means that you cannot be physically beaten or abused into giving a statement, and if you are, the statement may be thrown out by the court and may not be used against you. However, "MAY" is the key word. In order for you to suppress the statement, you would have a hearing called a **Miranda hearing**. At that hearing, a judge has to decide:

1. Whether or not force or threats of force were used against you AND

2. Whether such force or threat was so great that it compelled or forced you to confess or give a statement.

Unless, you can show some bruises in inappropriate places, a few broken ribs, black eyes that you didn't have before you were arrested...Motion DENIED. That statement is evidence against you.

The more common experience is the subtle coercion. Most of you, if you are ever arrested, think you know what time it is. You don't have a clue. You're in custody and trying to match wits with officers who have training and experience far beyond your little 15 to 25 years. So they tell you—

"We know it was you, if you admit it now, I'll talk to the judge to see if you can get a low bail." Yeah right! But you're half "zooted". So this works far more often than you think. He's lying and you better recognize it.

"Your boy is in the other room giving you up. Wanna hear what he said about you?" Your boy has probably said nothing, but they'll make something up if it gets you to talk, and understand, the law allows them to trick you, even lie to you.

"You are in big trouble and you need all the help you can get. You help me, I'll help you."

...And you're already scared. You know you need help; you're thinking about bail, your mom; this place (jail) is cold, it stinks, the food stinks...and did I mention that you're SCARED. Many confessions are gained by simple twisting of the facts and the little hook questions like those we just stated. The need for help is just as meaningful to someone who has been through the process before, but for someone who has never been in serious trouble, it is overwhelming. The person who has been "down" before, often is too smart for his own good. He's the guy who already has a story or defense made up, so he's ready to talk, and convict himself, before the police try to schmooze him. The result usually is...he gives his made up version. They don't believe him, but they take the statement down anyway. Then, he's ready to fall for all the usual bait. Now, if and when the defendant says anything close to what really happened, he is shown to be a liar, and a calculated criminal, by his own pre-planned statement.

Some helpful hints on questioning by police:

1. If you do not have a lawyer, do NOT answer any questions. This applies EVEN IF YOU ARE INNOCENT. The basic questions, such as, name, address, you are required to answer. Anything else is off limits. (And if your name and address are issues in your arrest, don't even tell them that). If you don't have a lawyer, you can request one. Once you request one, the questioning MUST stop. If it doesn't, your rights are being violated and you know these people mean you no good. What often happens is the officer will say something like, "the public defender will be here in the morning, but I won't, and right now I'm the only one who can help you." He's not on your side. Keep quiet.

2. If you have a lawyer, only answer questions in his/her presence. What good is it for you to have someone whose job it is to protect you, if you do not use him/her? You don't enter a war without your weapons. Criminal justice is war. Only answer what the lawyer tells you to answer and you'll be much better off.

3. If you are read your Miranda rights and do not want to be questioned, write that on the form.

I can't tell you how many cases I have been involved with where the defendant/client says: "I told them I didn't want to talk, but they kept asking questions so I just signed that form and they wrote down what they wanted." The form came in as evidence that they agreed to be questioned (and the signature on a copy of the statement or confession didn't help either). But what do you think would happen to that statement if the Miranda form had on it, "I don't want to answer any questions," next to your signature? You have a credibility call by a judge or jury that you can win.

4. If you are a juvenile (under 18-years-old) your parents

should be notified before you are questioned. The obvious way police get around that is the "non-custodial" questioning we talked about earlier. Juveniles should ask for a parent and a lawyer. Parents, when you get that call, do not go down to the precinct with your self-righteousness. I don't care how embarrassed you are, DO NOT allow that child to give a statement. One client's mother explained to me, "All I told him was 'just tell the truth.'" She believed the police when they told her that if Junior told them what happened, it would make things easier for him. She also believed that somehow Junior's conduct was reflecting negatively on her as a mother. Junior did as mom ordered and admitted to punching a man who was eventually beaten up by the juvenile's friends. During the beating, the man fell, hit his head on the curb and died. The statement was the only evidence the police had on 16-year-old Junior who is now doing 15 years in adult prison, 8 without parole.

5. If you are physically abused or emotionally distressed at the time you give a statement, let your lawyer know immediately. Don't wait until the day of your trial to tell your team that the police didn't play fair. Credibility is always an issue in court and the sooner you register a complaint, the more believable you are.

Back to our fact scenario. Let's assume that the drugs WERE Antoine's. What should he know? I am not telling you this to make you a better criminal. The truth is, the more you know, the more likely you will choose a straight path that does not include crime because you may get by once, twice, or three times, but the system is patient, it's not going anywhere. It's like slavery and welfare, it was made with you (minorities and poor people) in mind. Even for the biggest and best criminals, it only takes the system one time to get you and you're through!

The Fourth Amendment to the United States Constitution protects you from "**unreasonable searches and seizures**." **Searches** range from a mere pat down to a stripsearch. **Seizures** range from a simple stop for questioning to a full-blown arrest. The issue in a court is whether the action of the police is reasonable, given the circumstances, as he/she knows them to be.

Many street level drug dealers, when approached by the police, have a decision to make. "Should I run?" "Should I throw away what I have in my hand or pocket?" "Should I sit tight?" In our fact pattern, the drugs were dropped upon seeing the police. I don't know how many times a defendant has come to me and said, "When he arrested me, I didn't have anything on me." They believe they can "beat this case" because no drugs were found on them. DUH! Wrong, as two left shoes.

There are two major types of possession recognized under the law, **Actual** and **Constructive**.

Actual possession is when you have an item on you. You know what it is and you intend to control or have it. For example, when Antoine sees the police, he has two "clips" (twenty vials of cocaine) on him, in his hand, or in his pocket. He knows he has them and he knows what they are. If caught with them, he is in actual possession of CDS.

Constructive possession is when you do not have the object on you, but you know where it is or should be, you intend to exercise control over it and you have the ability to control or have it when you want to. The example that most often makes it to court is when a drug dealer hides his drugs under an abandoned porch or in a garbage can. When he needs to make a sale, he goes to the "stash" point, retrieves the items and puts the rest back. He is in constructive possession of the drugs in the stash point and can be convicted of possession even though the drugs are not on him. When you drop an illegal item, it's still yours and you can't even argue that you were illegally searched because the court will say you **abandoned** it or it was found in **plain view**. It wasn't on you, but you're "wearing it."

When these types of cases are prosecuted, the government will frequently rely on the alleged observations of a police officer. Credibility is always an issue. If a judge or jury believes the cop, you lose. If not, you walk. Seldom, is a defendant believed over the police.

These officers are trained on how to testify and what to testify to. They study the newest case law and are aware of making an impression in court. They have probably testified any number of times before and experience is the best teacher. Their position and their badge give them an air of respectability. How exactly do you attack the credibility of a police officer? Always remember that the police are human. They make mistakes, a lot of mistakes. As a defendant, you have to match the officer's credibility or catch him in an outright lie. Many times it takes both. Many times you lose even if you catch him lying. Again, to keep this on the real, I have only tried three cases in seventeen years where I believed that the officer was reporting the facts exactly as they happened.

Most of the time, they do NOT observe the alleged transfer of objects that led them to believe that a drug deal was taking place. Most of the time, they do NOT see the transfer of US currency, even though they report it that way. The police will tell you that street level drug deals are meant to be secret, but everything is observed out in the open. They are arresting kids who know a particular neighborhood like the back of their hands, yet when the police are spotted, they drop the drugs with a cop car 25 feet away. Happens...yes. But no where near as much as the incident where the police come into a neighborhood, line everyone up on a wall and search around until they find something. They know it's a high narcotics area and they are likely to find a "stash" or something that was dropped. So the real question is who is going to wear the drugs that will eventually be found? No one who is out there when they arrest the wrong guy is going to come to court and say it's the wrong guy. They have a credibility problem and there is the fear factor. The fear factor makes you ask, "If I say it wasn't his then they're going to ask me whose was it?" The correct answer to that question could cost you your life, so you keep quiet.

If you're lucky and you have some jurors from the hood who have experience with what the real deal on the street is, you have a shot. But most jurors have never heard of anything similar to the lifestyle of a street level drug deal and will side with the police no matter how insane a story he reports. The police and the criminal minded know one thing about the system that you do not. That is, it doesn't matter if the story you tell is true, even if you swear that it is. The story just has to be believable enough to convince twelve people.

Stereotypes, not facts, are the heart of the police investigation involving drugs. A group of black males is always a suspect class. It could be Boyz II Men, but if there is more than one black male and the harmony is not immediately present, the police will give their actions strict scrutiny. They testify in court that, "It is a high crime area." What makes it a high crime area? "The number of arrests made there." Interesting. It's not the number of convictions, but the number of arrests. So the statistics on crime do not reflect the fact that although five people were arrested in a drug raid, only one person was convicted of the drugs found there. The statistics that are offered in courts are deliberately inflated to portray certain communities as high crime areas.

Additional testimony may be, "They saw the police unit and began to walk away." Some communities call avoiding contact with the police, walking away, smart and prudent behavior. But in the minority community, it is suspicious behavior.

"The money in his possession was in denominations consistent with street level drug distribution." The police testify that anything from a one to a fifty dollar bill can be "proceeds" of drug transactions, making you a suspect, no matter how much money you have on you. Your style of dress, your handshakes, your language, are all subject to interpretation and have all been considered suspicious behavior.

What about the credibility of the defendant? If you have prior convictions, they will more than likely be entered into evidence against you, but can only be used if you testify and then, only for a jury to consider your credibility. The concept is silly, but it has been "upheld" by numerous courts. The premise is that a jury can consider a prior conviction to judge whether or not a person who has failed to conform to society's laws in the past, can be trusted to tell the truth about this case. A jury may not conclude that if you committed a crime in the past, you probably committed this one. I'm the lawyer and when a client comes to me and says I have a conviction, it's hard for me not to think that he probably didn't commit this one. But if he is on trial for this crime, what relevance is it that he was convicted four years ago of something else? You cannot even testify, as many defendants want to, by stating, "Hey, I pleaded guilty to that charge because I did it. I'm not pleading guilty to this one because I didn't do it."

The officer arresting you knows you from the neighborhood and knows you have a prior record. If you're set up by him, you can't even testify that he's lying without having your credibility attacked because of your prior record.

Also, you have as a defendant in a criminal trial, the presumption of innocence. Jurors never really understand that concept, but I like to explain it by saying: "When you come in the court, you have to believe that the defendant didn't do it. That means that the State has made a mistake or is outright lying." A jury should, with this concept in mind, give all doubts to the defendant, but they don't. Many times they engage in a balancing of credibility, as if the defendant has something to prove. A defendant can take the witness stand and lie through his teeth and there still can be reasonable doubt, if jurors understood the presumption of innocence.

Before I leave drug possession, I want you to understand a concept known as **joint possession**. Your typical case is an adult using a juvenile or a girlfriend to hold an illegal object or sell drugs for him. Just to show you the mindset, this person will allow the juvenile or girlfriend to hold the drugs, distribute the drugs, but the money is his. They convince these juveniles and/or some other "trying to be hard" kid that if they are caught with drugs, they won't do time or the system will be less harsh on them. Maybe, they'll get probation or community service. Joint possession means that one person is in actual possession of the illegal object while someone else, the adult, is in constructive possession. They both are in control and both can and will be found guilty. Unfortunately, with the girlfriend, many drug dealers will put their "stash" in her bag and never tell her it's there until it is time to start dealing. There are a lot of unwitting girlfriends in prison.

What I have tried to explain here is a very basic fact pattern on street level drug dealing. The reality is that the ways drugs are sold on the street are too numerous to outline. The result is almost always the same, jail, violence, no future and no hope. The rights that you have under the Constitution or legislature means nothing in the real world, if you don't recognize that life, liberty, and the pursuit of happiness means being free from random stops by police because you look suspicious or you shook hands with the wrong person in the wrong neighborhood. Call me a cynic, but I don't trust any police officer to report or testify to the whole truth. I have read too many reports that sound like the leading case from a law book to believe that the police do not tailor their reports and testimony to fit the cases they need. When I hear a police officer using legal terms, "Terry stop," "plain view," "exigent circumstances" I immediately think, "He's lying." Any reasonable examination of his testimony normally justifies my concerns. Unfortunately, the courts take each case one fact at a time and try to eliminate any form of argument that shows patterns of police misconduct on the street. So when I am about to take on a case that gives me a choice between the believability of a cop and the believability of a suspected drug dealer, generally, the jury is still out. One thing that is certain, given the choice between which one I want in my neighborhood, I'll take the cop. Most juries will too.

A Case of Rape

It's May. Spring is in the air and it's getting hot. All the girlies are beginning to dress down, minnies, daisy dukes (you know what I'm talking about). All the homeys are trying to get their "mack" on. It's like that in the spring. The best of times and the worst of times.

Picture it. Someone once said, that spring is the time for lovers. Fortunately, or unfortunately, depending on your perspective, even lovers have to be responsible, make good decisions. If you don't recognize what it is to be responsible, the system will make you see. When that happens, my telephone rings.

One evening, Raymond was coming home from school. He was hanging with his boys, "just kickin' it." They are approached by a group of girls. He knows most of them. One of them, Doris, goes with his best friend Carlos, so it's all good. There's small talk, laughing, joking, until Carlos pulls him aside.

"Yo Ray. See that 'G' over there? She wants to meet you."

"Ain't that the girl we saw at the park last week?"

"That's her. Check this out...she's Doris's cousin."

"No shit? Damn, she fine."

They meet. More small talk. He's impressed and is hoping that she is equally impressed. His boys are checking out every move he makes and he's trying to be cool. Not too silly, not too laid back. His boys are all over him.

"Yo Ray. Get the number."

"Yeah, and give it here. You know how we do Ray, we share."

"Yo, Ray? What should we tell Cheryl? You remember Cheryl don't you?"

He's hoping they back off; after all, there really is no "Cheryl."

But she doesn't seem to mind. It's about time to break and everyone is going their separate ways. She doesn't give up the number (Raymond believes she's playing the role) but, she says that she'll be at the party tonight, if he comes, maybe, he can have it then. Sounds like a plan.

By 7:00 p.m., Raymond is ready, but he is not going to the party until 10 p.m.; doesn't want to look too anxious. He has the car tonight. Mom is away on business and dad, a cop, works nights. Before he heads for the party, he grabs a "jimmy," puts it in his wallet, and now he's ready—in case he gets lucky.

It is about 10:15 p.m. when he arrives at the party and it's OFF THE HOOK. It takes about five minutes before Raymond spots Angie—that's her name…and she is all that. They talk, they dance, and it's nice; all evening it's nice. There's a little drinking, but not much. She's dressed sexy, but not "hoochie." Anyway, he's respectful. His parents raised him that way and she is easy to compliment.

At about 2:00 a.m., the party is breaking up and Doris suggests that they go somewhere to chill since she and Angie don't have to be home before 4:00 a.m. Raymond volunteers his home. They arrive at about 2:15 a.m. and Carlos and Doris immediately excuse themselves. They say they are going to the 7 Eleven for some cigarettes. Raymond and Angie are alone…at last.

No one knows what happened at the house, but when Doris and Carlos get back, it's about 3:45 a.m. and Angie is ready to go. She doesn't want to chitchat and will not stay in the house another minute—"Let's just go."

It's now about 6:30 a.m. and Carlos gets a call.

"How could your boy do something like that? Why didn't you tell me he was like that? Did he tell you what he did?"

"Hold up, mommi. You're talking too fast. Did what? Who?"

"You tell your boy I'm calling the cops on his tired ass."

"Yo. You buggin'. What's going on?"

"Ask your boy." (Phone slams).

Carlos immediately calls Raymond. Raymond's dad answers.

"Mr. Delgado, can I speak with Raymond?"

"Son, it's 6:30 in the morning... is everything alright? And so that you know, if everything is alright, you better think twice about calling here again at this time of the morning."

"Sorry, Mr. D. It is important."

"He's sleep, but hold on, I'll wake him up."

Mr. Delgado goes into Raymond's room to wake him. While he's shaking him, he notices some things that lead him to believe Raymond had company; female hairs in Raymond's brush, a female's bracelet, a torn open condom packet, two glasses on the night stand. Raymond wakes up.

"Teléfono, boy! By the way, I hope you didn't do anything foolish last night."

Mr. Delgado leaves the room.

"Hello?"

"Yo dog, what happened with you and Angie last night?"

"You called me for that? That's personal. What time is it anyway?"

"Dog! Doris called rippin' shit. Yo, she's talking about calling the cops."

"For what?"

"That's what I'm calling you for. Hold on."

Carlos calls Doris on his three-way.

"Hello."

"Yo, Boo. I got Ray on the line."

"Hello. It's me, Ray."

"You got some fuckin' nerve calling here. I can't believe you called here."

"Yo. Slow down. What...Why you blackin' out on me?"

"Slow down my ass. I introduce you to my cousin and you do something like this to her. I should kick your ass myself. The police will be here any minute and you won't get away with this!"

"Yo! Police? What are you talking about? What did I do?"

"You RAPED her!"

When Angie sits down with the police, she tells the following story:

After Carlos and Doris left her, Raymond showed her his home. He seemed like a nice guy and Doris said he was a good guy, so she felt comfortable with him. He was especially proud of his trophy case that was in his bedroom. While in the bedroom, he put on some soft music and asked her if she wanted to dance. They did. He began to tell her how beautiful she looked and how much he enjoyed being with her.

"Let's not let it end like this," he whispered.

The dance slowly turned into a grind. They kissed a lot. It was hot and heavy. He began to feel all over her, and she felt herself losing control of the situation.

"Stop!" she whispered. "Things are happening a little too fast for me." He eased up on the touchy feely, so she hoped that he had gotten the right message—but, they continued to kiss. After a few minutes, they stopped. He asked if she wanted something to drink. She laughed and said, "Si, something cold, it's hot in here." He laughed too. While he was out of the room, she used his brush to get her hair back together.

When Raymond returned, he had two glasses. She asked him what was in the glasses and he stated, "Pepsi with a touch of rum." She drank hers slowly. They talked and danced some more. During the talking, she remembers that he began to unbutton his shirt. "Don't get too comfortable," she mused. He said that he was just going to change shirts, but stopped to show her an "R" shaped tattoo he had over his heart. After more talking and dancing, he grabbed her hand and walked her to the bed. He began to undress her. She grabbed his hand away from her blouse on at least two occasions and stopped him from lifting her skirt.

"Stop! Raymond, Stop!" she said, as politely as she could under the circumstances. "Doris will be here any minute." "Relax, everything's gonna be alright," he said. But everything wasn't alright. She began to feel woozy. "I don't feel well," she said. But by now, they were on his bed, with him on top of her. "I said STOP!" she said angrily. But he wouldn't.

"I was scared and embarrassed. I didn't know whether to scream or fight. I began to cry. I kept saying, 'Please Raymond, don't. Stop Raymond please stop,' but he wouldn't. I began to lose control of my body. I wanted to fight, but I couldn't. I felt his knees separate my knees and I scratched his back and neck to get him to stop. He grabbed my hands and held them by my sides. Finally, I could feel him inside me, but I couldn't move, couldn't fight. I wanted to, but I couldn't. I just kept saying 'don't, please don't,' but he wouldn't stop. I just cried."

"When he finished, he kissed me on my cheek. Asked me if I was okay. He kept asking me that. I don't know what I said. I remember going into the bathroom and taking his brush to fix my hair. I locked the door behind me and prayed that Doris would get there soon. I still felt woozy and thought that I might pass out. I felt cheap. I just cried until Doris and Carlos came."

At approximately 9:00 a.m., Raymond and his father were awakened by a loud continuous knocking at the door. THE POLICE. They had a warrant to search the premises. Nothing that I say here can explain to you the sense of embarrassment and violation that a person with any sense of pride feels when total strangers are rummaging through your home. They go into your closets and your clothes; they are literally ripping up your world right in front of your eyes. They destroy your sense of man or womanhood, treating your most intimate and important possessions "like shit," and you they treat like you are worst than that. You want to stop it anyway you can, but all you can do is watch. Then again, nothing I say can explain to you the sheer sense of violation and helplessness, fear, and hatred of a victim of a rape.

Raymond was arrested, posted bail and spoke with his lawyer. He gave the following account—his side of the story:

"Carlos and Doris left Angie with me because they wanted to go get their thing off privately. I thought it would be okay because Angie and I had been having a real good time at the party and after. I figured that if something happened between me and Angie, I could handle it. If not...cool. I showed her almost every room in the house, except the bedrooms. Didn't want her to think anything was up. She said she heard I was a good basketball player, which I am, so I showed her my trophies, which were in my bedroom. She seemed impressed and wasn't uncomfortable about being in the bedroom."

"I put on some music so we could relax and talk, and we danced because we wanted to. We kissed because we wanted to. When things started to get heavy, she said, 'Stop' and we did. She kissed me first after that and we started heating up again. I stopped the second time. Honestly, I went to make sure I had my rubber, you know some protection, and to get us something to drink. We had a few drinks earlier and I thought a little something would make the mood just right. I got both of us colas and put a little rum in both glasses, but not a lot."

"When I came back in the room, we drank the drinks, kissed some more, and talked. After about a half an hour, I began to feel a little nice and relaxed. I took my shirt off. She said something, but I'm not sure what. I know that I showed her my tattoo, which she touched, and that's when I grabbed her hand and we walked across the room to my bed. She didn't resist. The conversation was good, the dancing was good, the kissing was good, so I'm thinking, it's all good. She said she felt a little woozy, but I just assumed that she was feeling as nice as I was."

"I began to unbutton her top and feel her breasts, but she grabbed my hands. I laid her down and began to lift her skirt. At first she said, 'Stop'. But then she said, 'Don't Stop!' I didn't stop because we were having a good time and we both wanted to do this. During the sex, she scratched me and moaned a lot. Again saying, 'Stop and Don't Stop'. All of this was exciting to me and I thought it was just as good to her."

"I didn't RAPE anyone."

Far too many people find themselves in a fact pattern similar to this one. The decisions you make can and often do affect you for the rest of your life. It will affect you whether you are a victim of the rape, of the allegation, or of the system that will eventually make your decision irrelevant.

The proper legal term for the crime charged is **sexual assault** or **aggravated sexual assault**. It is simply unlawful penetration or sexual contact. Unlawful means that the victim is not in agreement with the sexual contact which regularly means he/she said NO. The degree of the charge is dependent upon how much force and injury was placed on the alleged victim and/or the vulnerability of the victim. Sexual assault is usually a second degree offense, and in many jurisdictions, a person convicted of this crime faces a maximum of 10 years in prison with a presumed 7 year term. That means, you could do 7 years before you're even eligible for release.

The assault becomes **aggravated sexual assault** when the force used in the crime is the critical element or when the perpetrator is in a position of power, authority, or familial relationship with the victim. Depending on the amount of the force and the jurisdiction you are in, you could get 20 years to life, if convicted. Once convicted of either of these offenses, a defendant is subject to any number of sentences including having his name registered in a sex offender hotline; having his name registered with the local authorities (and published to the community); or serving the sentence in a center for the treatment of sex offenders.

How will Raymond defend this case?

"**Consent**" often is the defense in a sexual assault case. The reason is simple. Frequently, there is a consensual aspect of the incident and a credible defendant wants to convince a jury that he's no "sex-crazed" animal, which often is the perception of rapist. He obviously cannot say it wasn't him; she can identify him, and by now the DNA and other scientific evidence have matched him to her.

What makes up consent? Consent means that she agreed to have sex with him. She was in her right mind, of age, and was a willing participant. In other words, she was "down with it."

From the door, we know that they had been drinking. Let's assume that her blood alcohol level was high. The prosecutor is going to call some expert witness or doctor who will testify that the blood alcohol level was so high that she was drunk or as close to drunk as one can get.

What difference does that make? When you are drunk and/or in some instances "high," you cannot consent (agree) to have sex. You are not in your right state of mind and many jurisdictions eliminate consent as a defense, if the victim is intoxicated. Sorry, Raymond. It also doesn't help Raymond that he gave Angie that cola with a "little rum." It looks like he was trying to drug her, NOT relax her. A jury looking at that along with the fact that she never says, "let's do this" and there being no sex act before the cola, could, and often does, find NO CONSENT.

What if she's under age? Can't consent. Don't even ask.

Many of you so-called "pimps" out there are sleeping with these 12 to 16-year-old girls who act like they're 20. Get a life!!! She can't, as a matter of law, consent to sex if she is 14-years-old or under. Further, in most jurisdictions, if she is under 17 years with a sex partner four years older, he'd better keep a plane ticket in his pocket. (She's 14 and her "man" is 23. She gets pregnant. Mom wants to know, who's the daddy? You've heard the expression…"under the jail?" That's where mom and the prosecutor want "the baby's daddy").

One client came to me crying because the father of the girl he was sleeping with was pressing charges of statuary rape against him. **Statutory rape** simply means that the State has to prove that the defendant had sex with a minor. Having confessed to the sex act, he said it should not be treated as a crime because they were in love. The fact that she was 15 and he was 30 seemed unimportant to him. He was upset when I negotiated a probationary term for him, if he were to plead. His anger subsided a bit when I allowed him to tell his story to my female staff, all of whom called him a sick pervert. The reality set in that a jury might also see him that way and probation began to look better than 10 years in prison.

The issue of consent doesn't address the maturity of the young girl. It does address the legislative belief that at certain ages a young person should not and cannot make this decision.

The same is true for someone who is mentally retarded. The court will look to see if they have the mental capacity to consent. They may be of age, but if a court determines that the mental state is under age, it's time for the sex partner to pack the toothbrush.

Probably the case that is as old as time and is the hardest to defend is the child victim. Often, these trusting little 8-year-olds are confused by the type of attention they are getting when someone (usually an adult) approaches them sexually. However, when the confusion ends or the pain is too much for them to bear, they will tell someone. No one is more believable in court than a young child who says, "He put his pee pee right here and it hurt. ...but, he told me not to tell mommy." And no one is more despised by juries, judges, and lawyers than a child molester. (You're paying this lawyer to represent you and he's thinking you're a sick pervert. Do you really think you are getting his best effort?).

"All I did was feel her booty." Touching someone in an inappropriate place for the purpose of sexual arousal or gratification is a crime. Oftentimes, juveniles come to me with this one liner and I tell them the same thing the court will when they are convicted. "Control yourself."

Young ladies, however, should not be fooled by our fact scenario. Convicting Raymond is not a simple task. Raymond thinks he did nothing wrong and often these matters come to trial. Raymond is on his way to college, and a good-looking young man. His father is a police officer. He's in the top one-third of his class and all the girls at school like him. The teachers think he is a great kid and very respectful. So credibility is a question. Who are you going to believe? Jurors are human beings and frequently these cases come down to people's perceptions. Most people view "rape" as that violent act by some "sex-crazed animal" and they come to court looking for any sign of that from the defendant. Sometimes it surfaces, but with Raymond's background and some good "lawyering," the female has to fight uphill against this perception.

"I just can't believe that a nice boy like that, with all that he has going for him, would do something like that." Perception in a nutshell equals William Kennedy Smith (medical school student, member of the Kennedy family; white) not guilty vs. Mike Tyson (boxer, violent history; black) guilty.

Everyone has a perception of what a rapist looks like. Five "white" boys from Glen Ridge, New Jersey are accused of raping a mentally retarded girl. It's called a "gang bang." It's rape. Sadly, it happens everyday. Young boys caught up in their own sense of group power and entitlement, believing that the girl wants it or won't tell. Young fools begging for prison and thinking with "the wrong head." The judge grants them bail pending appeal following their conviction. No one in the court can believe that such a serious offense could be treated so "cavalierly" by the court. But the perception generated by some very good "lawyering" was that these "good kids" were not a flight risk or a threat to themselves or others. The community in Glen Ridge seems to be accepting of it. The family of the retarded rape victim thinks differently. (By the way, I have never seen such a perception extended to a black or Latin defendant charged with rape. Often, affluence, money, and community support creates the perception that benefits a defendant and often minorities lack these privileges in a criminal setting. It is the way of the world that the color of privilege is white).

The part of a rape case that often seems to lack humanity is the job the defense attorney is going to do in attacking the alleged victim's credibility. I believe in my client's position and I am duty bound to show the jury that this so-called victim is a liar. Maybe she is a "hoochie" or maybe an embarrassed little girl who got in over her head and doesn't have the courage to admit it, even if it costs Raymond his life. Or maybe, if my client is a celebrity, she's a gold digger.

"Even YOU thought that Raymond was a perfect gentleman, didn't you?"

"You wanted to dance with him; you wanted to kiss him; you wanted to see his trophies; you wanted to be in his bedroom; you wanted something to drink; you knew it had rum in it; you wanted the sex, DIDN'T YOU?"

Ladies! You have never had an experience like being questioned by a skillful attorney who is out to prove you are the bad guy. You have to handle it and it's much tougher than the limited questioning we just went through. It's intense. It's your credibility versus his credibility with a defense attorney on his side who is coming for your throat with all the skill and tenacity he/she possesses. Jurors are trying to judge, but they can reasonably believe everything you say and still find that there is a reasonable doubt as to a defendant's guilt on the charge of sexual assault or aggravated sexual assault.

Rape is SERIOUS. It is a serious invasion of someone. Don't take sex and/or sexual activity as a game. The flirtation, the kissing, the touching, the willingness to be left alone are all evidence to be used against you at trial, and it will be.

"Tell me, if you will, Angie, is my client a good kisser? I mean did you like kissing him?"

"At first, yes."

"At first? Was there a time when you stopped liking the kissing of my client?"

"Yes."

"So you're saying that you kissed him even though you didn't like it?"

"No."

"Well, would it be safe to say that the only time you began to dislike my client's kissing is when you reached the point that you describe as him forcing himself on you?"

"You can say that."

"OK, I will. And at that time he tried to kiss you, that is while he was on top of you and inside of you. Correct?"

"Yes."

"And according to you, he's forcing himself on you, but you still kiss him even though you didn't like it."

"I'm not saying that."

"Anyway, when you liked the kissing, did you have your arms around him?"

"Yes, in the beginning."

"And you rubbed his back, didn't you?"

"Yes."

"And you rubbed his back hard, didn't you?"

"Yes. But when I felt I was losing control, I stopped and told him to stop."

"And there was some grinding of your bodies together, correct?"

"Yes."

"And that was something that you liked for a while, right?"

"Yes."

"By the way, do you always grind when you dance with someone or kiss them?"

"OBJECTION!"

"I'll move past it, Judge."

"That's a good idea, counselor."

"Angie, tell me about the dress you were wearing that night. Did you and Doris pick that dress out for you prior to going to the party?"

"Yes, we did."

"And that dress that the two of you picked out, you did so because you both thought it made you look sexy, I think 'hot' was the word Doris used, correct?"

"Yes."

"And there was even some discussion between you and Doris that if Raymond saw you in that dress, quoting Doris now, 'he'd be all over you.'"

"I didn't mean rape me."

"Well, you got dressed with him 'all over you' on your mind and that night, that's exactly what you wanted and exactly what you got, nothing more, nothing less."

"You're wrong."

"Isn't it a fact that you and Doris not only discussed how to turn my client on, how you should walk, your perfume, your hair, but you discussed the fact that she would leave the two of you alone and you could do what you wanted to do all along, right, sleep with my client?"

"NO!"

"Sure, you did and the only one who was clueless in this was my client."

"OBJECTION."

"Tell me this young lady, when he was inside you, did you rub his back then?"

"No, I scratched his back."

"Oh yeah, right. You scratched his back in the same spot that you were rubbing hard while you were grinding before you decided to have sex. Right? The same area, correct?"

"I'm not answering that."

"No problem. Answer this. Did you observe that there was a 7 Eleven store two blocks away from Raymond's home?"

"Yes."

"They sell cigarettes there, don't they?"

"I guess so."

"So how long do you think it would take to buy a pack of cigarettes and walk to Raymond's house? At best, five minutes?"

"I guess so."

"And Doris left you alone with Raymond for what, an hour and a half?"

"About that."

"Hmm. Sounds like a plan to me."

"OBJECTION."

"Withdrawn."

Fortunately, courts have stumbled through "**Rape Shield Laws**" which attempt to protect victims from having their entire sexual history exposed in court. Defense attorneys can no longer probe into all of a victim's sexual episodes to show that they are sexually active. But being smart, being honest with yourself, and keeping out of these situations, is the best protection. Please don't tell me about men or boys needing to learn how to control themselves. That's probably true, but it is not happening. So get off your moral high horse and get with the real!

This is just one case scenario. You will hear about it over and over, in college and in high school; at the office party or after the basketball game. Sex is everywhere. Just remember, NO means NO, but it means so much more in public than it does in private.

I have chosen for my own reasons to deal with this type of sexual assault case. Frankly, ladies, the person who is most likely to rape you is someone you know and possibly someone you trust. It will be your husband or boyfriend, your father or your uncle, your religious leader or your teacher. This unfortunate set of circumstances makes your decision to come forward AND TELL even more difficult. You hate and love in the same breath. You wonder if you tell how it will impact on HIS life or the family. Most often, you tell a family member and the fact that they find it hard to believe makes you wonder if it was your fault. ("Uncle Joe? He would never do something like that."). Just remember Uncle Joe, rape is a crime and someday she will tell someone who will believe her. Many of the "Uncle Joes" that I meet are in the system because two or three familiars, family members or school girls (sometimes school boys) have claimed the same thing. And with the advent of DNA (whatever that is) you can't hide forever.

Finally, you all know about the "sexual predator" who grabs some unsuspecting female, drags her somewhere secluded and rapes her at knife or gun point. This is an act of violence from a sick, angry, dangerous individual. My files lead me to believe that these guys are not necessarily looking for sex. They are looking for power, fear, control, or pain to get them off. Hopefully, you know the rules. Stay out of secluded/dark areas (the woods, back alleys); don't talk to strangers privately; lock your doors; travel in groups or with someone else; and always let someone know when you are going to be out late. Finally, remember that in this type of situation, your mission is to stay alive. Take every precaution and live to testify.

Little Girls and Boys...and their Toys

Greater minds than mine have struggled with trying to understand why violence is so endemic to the fabric of American society. Don't be fooled. It didn't start with the death of Tupac or Biggie. It has been with us since day one, and quiet as it is kept, it's not just a "black" problem. No time in history was more violent than that of the African slave trade. No home built in this country is free from the violence that it took to uproot and eliminate the Native American. Almost every group of immigrants to arrive on American soil is equipped with their stories of violence in the pursuit of the American dream. The study of American history is an essay either on the exercise of brute force by the powerful or a statement on the failure of diplomacy. Today, in the courts, it's a statement on toys in the hands of kids too immature to know what a good decision is, let alone, its consequence. It's emotion gone mad. Unfortunately, it seems that it has always been that way.

It's a gray day. Raining, nasty, cold. The telephone rings at the office.

"Counselor, I need your help."

"What's happening? What's the problem?"

"The police just arrested my son. They say he shot someone. He's at the jail."

A telephone call is immediately placed to the police department.

"Hello, It's my understanding that you are holding X. I am his lawyer. Can you please let everyone involved know that he has counsel and will not be giving any further statements. If he is being questioned, please stop now. I'll be there in 10 minutes. Also, please make a note of the time of my call so that the record is clear."

When I arrive at the police precinct, I immediately begin to seek out the client's son. He's 17-years-old and charged with **murder**—the intentional killing of another. We meet. We talk.

Please understand one thing about this system. Once you get involved with the criminal justice system, you have lost complete control of your life. The life that you thought you had and the freedom you took for granted is gone from day one. You think it's like television and all the problems are worked out in an hour, with only a few commercial interruptions. Not so! You are that fly in the spider web. You walked in and often it costs you your life to get out.

"Mr. Bash, can you get me out of here? Maybe get my bail lowered?"

"Son, what do you know about bail? Do you know what you are charged with?"

"Yes. But I don't want to just sit in jail until I get a trial."

By now, I have made my initial assessment of the defendant. He's lost. In most jurisdictions, **homicide** (murder) is a mandatory 30 years to life prison sentence. He's worrying about making bail. Wake Up! Most courts will deliberately set his bail out of his range so that he has to sit in jail. After all, they argue, "you are a threat to others and maybe yourself."

People have the cynical perception that defense attorneys are in court everyday making up defenses in order to get bad people off. Some do, but the majority of defense attorneys take the facts as they come and ask two questions that help them decide how to defend a case. One, do the facts submitted by the State support the charge? Two, do the facts support proof beyond a reasonable doubt? I always ask myself the first question because I know that in many cases the government overcharges. That is, they charge a higher crime and then bargain at the level of the crime they truly believe they can prove. This concept is hard for a lay person to understand, so I'll explain.

A person is charged with **1st degree murder** for shooting another. The facts in the possession of the government show that there is a potential provocation that will reduce the charge to **manslaughter** or **2nd degree murder**, but the defendant is charged with the 1st degree crime anyway. The 1st degree charge comes with a life imprisonment term and the client is left to try to seek a deal on the manslaughter or go to trial and face life, if he loses. Had he been charged with manslaughter only, he would face 10 to 30 years and would be willing to take the risk at trial. But he's not willing to risk life, if the plea offer changes to manslaughter and the recommended sentence is 10 years in prison with 5 years without parole. It's the horse's head in the bed; the offer you can't refuse.

The second question is based on my overview of the case. I am trying to figure out if I can beat this case and my assessment comes from the facts presented by the government. If I can dissect the government's case without ever having to look deeply into the client's version of the facts, the government is in serious trouble. I take this path because in most cases the defendant is not going to testify. He or she may have prior convictions that I don't want the jury to hear about. Jurors say they are not prejudice, but one of the most common prejudices in the court system is people's belief that if you committed a crime in the past, you probably will commit another. Every judge sentencing a defendant finds, as an aggravating factor, this exact proposition and it is hypocritical to think that jurors do not.

I then have to make an assessment of the client; check out his mannerisms, his speech, his walk, his dress. Is he afraid? Is he intelligent? Is he new at this? Has he been through this before? He may be inarticulate, unable to communicate his story in a way that the jury will understand. He may be hot-tempered or appear cold-blooded, as if he doesn't care. I have to make these assessments if I am really concerned about defending him. If your attorney in a criminal matter, is talking about going to trial and hasn't formed some opinion about you as a witness or an opinion about the strengths of the government's facts, you better get your train ticket because the "railroad" is coming.

However, I have assessed the crime as well. This case was a homicide. **Homicide** is the intentional killing of another. A homicide becomes a **murder** when that intentional killing has no justification. When it has no justification, you should know that it is equal to suicide. Why would I say that? If you kill someone intentionally, you are basically saying, "take my life too."

The defendant was standing in the hallway at school talking to some friends. The deceased went to that high school as well. On the day of the shooting, the victim was late to class. He was running down the hall when he accidentally bumped into the defendant, knocking him down. He apologized, but as most young wrong-headed boys do, the defendant took it personally.

"Yo. Punk, Watch where you going next time."

"Yo man I said I was sorry. You alright?..."

"FUCK that! I should knock your stupid ass out. Punk ass."

I asked him, "Why didn't you just drop it right there?"

"You just can't let people diss' you. My father taught me that you have to stand up to people."

"Did he tell you that it's sometimes better to walk away?"

"Then everybody will think I'm a punk."

"So what! Why do you care about what people think?"

"My father said if they think you're a punk, they'll keep getting in your face."

"Do you think your father was teaching you to kill someone?"

"I didn't intend to kill him.... If a sucker's coming for me, he gets what he gets."

"Something else you learned from dad?"

"Yeah."

"Well, what happened next?"

"Sucker said, something like he ain't no punk."

At this moment, I'm thinking, "Why didn't the victim just drop it?" Maybe, he's trying to sound tough too and not get "dissed." Maybe he has a dad out there locked into the reality of the 1970s as well. The client continued.

"I swung on him right there. We tussled for a while and the principal broke us up. I was gonna squash it, but I heard he was looking for me after school. So I went looking for him and I was ready."

"Whose gun was it?"

"My dad's."

It only took one shot to end the two lives. The victim died instantly. The client gave his life away to keep from being "dissed." There is this mistaken notion out in the world that being "dissed" is something worth killing over. There is also this foolish belief that you can "step to" someone and gain respect. Most of these kids with guns are shooting first because they can't handle a real problem or make a good decision. They are scared as hell of anyone and anything, and the gun, they think, makes them strong, gives them "juice." Don't believe me? The next time some "thug" wants to kill someone or take his gun to a party, tell him he can beat the boy in a fair one. He will literally pee in his pants at the thought. The next time some "troubled" kid (whatever that is) tells you he's going to kill everyone in the school who "dissed" him, tell him that would make him the punk that they say he is, not a hero, and you'll steal the 15 minutes of fame he's really seeking and maybe save a life or two. I know this sounds simplistic, but often it is just that simple.

There once was a time when young "fellas" were "beefin," they would have a fight after school. Often, this would resolve the issue. With a fight, it is seldom that one person is totally outclassed; beaten senseless. You gained your respect simply because you stood up and if you got in that one lucky punch, you could end up the day as "the MAN." In a fight, both parties could walk away with some dignity. My boys always thought I won the fight. His boys always thought he won. Both he and I left the fight too beat up and tired to argue again. He earned my respect and I earned his. Not today. Every parent with a sense of respect for the time needs to understand that now the manhood game is played with toys.

A handgun is the toy of choice. Any punk can get his hands on one and considering how few young people possess problem solving skills, life and death becomes an instant consideration.

"J" scored 30 points in a basketball game. After the game, he took five bullets because he was talking trash during the game.

"D" had a fist fight with his best friend "W" over a girl that didn't really want either one of them. "D" loss the fight. He came back with a nine millimeter handgun. "W" took five bullets.

"N" broke up with "M." "M" went and got his gun. Three bullets hit "N" (one in the head) but she survived and two of the bullets hit "N's" Aunt "R" who died instantly.

A confrontation over drug turf erupts. The losers return and spray the corner with bullets. They miss the rival drug dealers (they always do) and kill an elderly grandmother who is trying to save her two small grandchildren from the gunfire.

The one thing that is consistent in each of these cases is the toy of choice in the hands of people who let their emotions rule over reason. In a strict ghetto definition... "a punk." In the hood, if you want to feel like you have something going on when you know that you have nothing to offer, you get a gun. The gun gives you a sense of power that makes you feel important when normally you would be the neighborhood cornball, nerd, or even "bitch."

Most of the time when someone responds with a handgun, he or she just didn't take that extra minute to think the problem through. Many times it is because they do not have that ability. You spend your entire 15 to however many years learning how to resolve conflict and in one emotion-filled moment, you forget everything and it costs you your life. Every day of your life, up until the time of that drastic, emotional, life-altering decision, you have been taught to make good decisions. "Look first before you cross the street." "Beware of strangers." "Stop for a red light." "Shake hands and walk away." "Do unto others as you would have them do unto you." For too many young people, these "lessons" on decision-making sound stupid, but they follow them everyday. Your parents and teachers taught you these "stupid" little lessons, and thousands more, to drive home a greater point. "Think before you act."

Females are not immune from this problem. There are an increasing number of females who act violently because of a minor provocation and their inability to think a problem through. Although, you may not see as many female shooting incidents (unfortunately they are increasing), it appears that their weapon of choice often is the razor or boxcutter.

"I cut her because she thinks she's cute."

"That bitch is sleeping with my man."

Their problem is often the same as their male counterparts; lack of common sense and social skills. Emotion that overrules common sense will always result in bad decisions, which often leads to violence.

I've been to too many crime scenes and funerals, looked into the eyes of too many mothers, children, and victims who just want to understand why their son or daughter had to die. I am an attorney and my job is to represent the person charged. Attorneys seldom try to understand the reason why a violent act occurs and when we do, it is only to figure out the best defense strategy. We are professionals lost in the profession.

Do you understand that in your anger, you gave away your own life and destroyed countless others? Do you understand that somewhere out there is a mother who loved her child, a son or daughter who loved their father, mother, brother, or sister? You weren't man or woman enough to just squash it, so all of your lives were destroyed. Mom and dad were trying to teach you to stand up for yourself, but not to kill (I hope). Standing up means making a good decision and often the good decision is to leave it alone no matter how mad you think you are.

In many cases, the unfortunate truth is that the parents need Decision Making Skills 101 as well. So the child is in deep trouble with you as a role model and, mom and dad, "If you don't know you better ask somebody" too. Parents cannot use the strategy of yesterday on this generation of children. And this generation of parents is so unprepared for the job that many of these kids don't really stand much of a chance. A child is disrupting the class. She's cussing out the teacher, creating all types of problems, until one day the teacher grabs her up. Maybe she snatches the little brat by her collar or maybe gives her a failing grade. Mom comes to school the next day. She should be in the teacher's corner or at least give her the benefit of the doubt. She should believe that the teacher is interested in the best for her child, maybe innocent until proven guilty. She should address the teacher with some respect, and if she thinks the teacher was wrong, at least be an example of what's right for her child. But that doesn't happen. Mom and the daughter cuss the teacher out together and kick her behind up and down the stairs. They can't believe that they are being treated like criminals when the police arrest them both, or that their little girl is not the victim. She is a victim. A victim of some unprepared, uneducated, misguided parents. She's on the road to destruction and mom is her chauffeur.

Acts of violence range from **simple assault** to **homicides** (murder/manslaughter). The vast majority of these actions occur in what is referred to in the law as the "**heat of passion**." Something happens to get you "fired up" and you act on it. Each of these acts of violence requires that you intend some violence. Example: Some guy accidentally bumps into my car. I get mad. (I don't think it through). I get out of my car and smack him. This act is simple assault because I intended to hit him. The State must prove that I intended to cause **bodily injury**, which frequently means hurt or discomfort.

Let's assume that I get out of the car and beat the guy up. Depending upon the nature of my attack and the injury to the other guy, I would more than likely be charged with **aggravated assault**. **Aggravated assault** means I intended to cause **substantial or serious bodily injury**, that is, injury that causes lost of a bodily function, severe pain or serious harm.

As you can see, the charge is usually commensurate with the intention, the injury and the violence. So is the penalty in a court of law. Same example, and I get out of my car with a baseball bat. The use of the weapon can change the behavior from aggravated assault to **attempted murder**.

Finally, if the toy of choice is a handgun and I shoot the gentleman, murder is the charge if and when he dies. The degree of the murder charge is generally determined by the nature of the provocation. If you are legitimately provoked (James came home and found his wife in the bed with his neighbor; Evelyn was being physically beaten daily by her husband) the provocation will usually mean that you will be charged with manslaughter or murder in the second degree. If you "lie in wait" for someone or plan to kill someone, or even if you kill with willful and wanton disregard for the value of human life, you may face first degree murder and often, in many states, the death penalty.

The client says, "I didn't intend to kill him. I was just trying to scare him." When you use a weapon in an act, the law presumes that you intend the consequences of your using it. Simply put, you begin your trial by having everyone who will judge you believing that you intended to kill the victim. In most criminal prosecutions, intent is an element of the crime that the prosecution must prove and you don't want to give it away. You are required to rebut (challenge) the presumption and if you do not, then you are out of luck. You can usually rebut a presumption by telling a jury what your true intention was. In other words, you testify. It is not as easy as it looks and often you make or break a case out of your own mouth.

The usual stereotypes and prejudices go into the attorney's consideration of whether or not to have you testify. Are you articulate? Are you an idiot? How will the jury perceive you? Are you likely to get confused and look like you are lying? Those who have a little more education, often make better witnesses. It is not enough that you know what happened or what you want to say. It often boils down to how and how well you say it. Most attorneys do not want to put a defendant on the witness stand if they don't have to.

Sometimes, the reason they put a defendant on the witness stand is because they have no choice or they have nothing to lose. Putting a defendant on the witness stand, often is a last resort. You "wannabe" criminals think you are being put on the witness stand because you are a star, when in fact, the attorney is thinking, "You're damn near convicted, so let's take a shot at you testifying. We have nothing else to give the jury."

On a few occasions, I have had defendants who I had no problem with putting on the witness stand. I have to decide if they can handle it. Their protestations or insistences have no place in my consideration. I am looking for the defendant who is innocent and it shows in his fire, his energy, and his body language. Also, the story he is about to tell, must be factually compelling, giving a jury some reason to doubt the story postured by the government. Finally, he or she better be able to tell the story preferably in English with as little or as much "flava" as needed. Acts of violence are so random and life-altering, that it is often hard for a jury to make sense of your conduct in a "civilized" society.

Another interesting dilemma is that as attorneys we measure victories differently from defendants. Most attorneys, who see a defendant facing life in prison or maybe the death penalty, are happy with a jury verdict or plea to a **lesser-included offense**. Frequently, the facts dictate an argument and conclusion for manslaughter or criminally negligent homicide as opposed to murder; assault as opposed to aggravated assault. So when you say, "I didn't intend to kill him, I was just trying to scare him," understand that even then you may have 8 to 15 years in prison to think about what you didn't intend. In case no one ever told you, that is called a consequence.

"It was an accident." Depending on the weapon used and the manner of its use, accidents can eliminate the intent required to injure or kill. Further, under the right circumstance, "accident" can be an absolute defense that may lead to your complete exoneration.

For example, assume that the defendant was driving his vehicle and accidentally strikes someone with it. The victim dies. This is an accident. Or, assume that the defendant found his father's gun. He is showing it to a friend when it discharged, injuring the friend. Again, an accident.

In the first scenario, most defendants are not customarily prosecuted. Accidents happen and most courts will recognize that. However, what if the driver has been drinking or using drugs? It's still an accident, but now the government can demonstrate that your intoxication shows **reckless disregard for the safety of others** or **criminal negligence**. Where there is no intent to injure or kill, recklessness or negligence replaces intent. The accident becomes a prosecution that often leads to a conviction, another bad decision and another full prison cell.

Similarly, with our second fact pattern, the defendant wants to show that he did not know that the gun was loaded and he did not have the intention to shoot anyone. Remember, the law presumes that you intended the consequences of the use of the gun. The consequence of the use of a gun is someone getting shot. In this case, the victim lived to tell the prosecutor that it was an accident and therefore the defendant was not prosecuted for the shooting. If the victim had died, it would have been a different story.

Doesn't there have to be a motive for a killing? Good question. Simply stated, NO. The government in a homicide does not have to prove a motive. Motive is evidence that can be used against you, or lack of motive is evidence that the defense can use to show accident, lack of intent or innocence. Motive is not an element of the charge against you and you can be convicted without any motive being offered.

What if I am defending myself? Another good question.

Self-defense is recognized as a defense in almost every jurisdiction. However, self-defense is only acceptable if you are in immediate danger (or reasonably believe that you are in immediate danger), if you use the amount of force necessary to repel the danger and the force you use is not in excess of the danger presented to you. These questions are always fact sensitive. They often come down to which facts a jury believes. "I thought he had a gun, so I shot him first before he shot me." "He swung on me, so I was protecting myself." "I was scared. He was so much bigger than me, so I grabbed a knife." Each of these statements made up the basis for a successful self-defense argument. Unfortunately, I can point to each one of these statements as being an unsuccessful self-defense claim as well.

In our original fact pattern, the kid and his father agreed to defend his case by arguing that he shot the victim because he reasonably believed that he was in immediate danger. The victim had a history of fights and was known to carry a knife. Because of the victim's known history, the prosecutor offered the client a plea bargain to manslaughter and 10 to 15 years in prison. I recommended that he take it. In order to win at trial, the defendant would have to testify. I could not penetrate that part of his hard head and convince him that trying to sound or look "ghetto hard" was not going to help him in the jurisdiction he would be tried in. He refused the plea. He refused to take the braids out of his hair. He refused the suit in favor of Phat Farm. After all, his father told him to be himself. "Yo!" We lost at trial.

In this business, you often want to help for the sake of helping, but the cardinal rule of a criminal defense attorney is, "get paid." You know that people come to you seeking your advice and expertise, but far too often, they have a perception of justice that your advice cannot penetrate. To defend a person accused of a violent crime requires that you try to see the client as a jury might see him or her because violent crime is judged every day in the courts, the press, and on street corners. People are frightened by violent crime. Additionally, most people are frightened by young people. And if you are black, forget about it. When you get involved in this kind of activity, you better understand that most jurors don't really want to hear your side. They see bullet holes in a body and it scares the hell out of them. Most jurors are horrified by the thought that the victim's face was slashed and she received 27 stitches regardless of what your defense is. They don't get a chance to see you the way your father does, neither will the attorney. He's through with you and on to the next fee. Unless of course, you have another 15 grand for an appeal.

So reality finally sets in. The rage/emotion that you thought you felt that caused you to act violently, has turned to tears. Daddy's way of thinking "back in the day" doesn't matter. You had a decision to make and you messed up in a way that you can't take back. You have been in jail for two years waiting for trial. You cry a lot now. You smell bad, you hate jail, you can't see your girl, and none of your people will accept your collect calls. The prosecutor offers you 15 years to plead guilty (you will probably do 5 to 10 years). Your options are narrowing. Go to trial, win and you go home. Lose and get 30 years in prison. Plea and be home in 5 to 10 years.

It is your decision to make, not your mother's or your father's. You are a man or a woman under the law, if you are old enough to hurt someone. If you ever learn anything from your parents, I hope you learn that all decisions have a consequence. Isn't it ironic? If you had made a good decision in the beginning, just squashed it, walked away, worked it out, "left all the drama to Denzel," there would have been no need for the next decision.

On the day of this client's sentencing, the judge "blacked out" on the client and told him that the next time he sleeps in his own bed or eats at McDonald's, he will be 50 years old ... at least. Now that's DISSING!!!

A Few Stolen Moments

At times, I sit in courtrooms around the country and wonder what level of divine justice there must be that brings certain people into this system. Many times the criminal does not get caught. Many times he does. Sometimes the criminal is too smart for his own good and that gets him into the system. At other times, he is so dumb that getting caught is a forgone conclusion.

Every year, in one jurisdiction, the police call up felons who are fugitives and tell them that they won Super Bowl tickets. You cannot imagine how many of these intellectual giants rush into the arms of the police thinking that there is something out there for nothing. How about the criminal who decides he's going to visit some 14-year-old he met online? His intention is to have sex with her. He later finds out she has been in contact with the authorities, not because she wanted to (because a lot of the babies online are down with the meeting), but because her parents caught her. So he walks into prison to satisfy a "jones" he could easily satisfy in the 30 and older chatrooms.

Sometimes, I think that people get what they deserve in this system, but I know better.

Even if you are the most hardened criminal or just plain stupid, you deserve the best of what the system has to offer. Unfortunately, the system is not equipped to give you what you deserve, "equal justice under the law." When you have been in the system for a while and you have seen how the laws change with political attitudes, you begin to believe, as I do, that the law is targeting groups of people, not necessarily the conduct that is criminal.

Any competent judge, prosecutor, and defense attorney can balance the equities in any criminal matter and resolve it without mandatory terms, three strikes laws, or enhanced penalties being imposed on them. They all know that if you are rich, you can avoid a lot of the process. If you are white, you can avoid a lot of the process. And if you are both, this process was not made for you anyway, so what are you doing here? If you lack any of the "privileges," often all you can hope for is some divine intervention. When you are a part of the process, you learn to fear that type of justice more than you do the system.

Scott was a thief. His friends, growing up, were into cars and heavy metal music. It struck me as odd when I met him that he was sitting in the county jail with penny loafers on, a button down shirt, and reading the Wall Street Journal. It was more odd when you consider all the indicia of "privilege" that I don't normally see was topped by the fact that Scott was white. His father used to brag that someday Scott would join his law firm and as a kid Scott had every advantage life could offer.

When I first met Scott, he was typical of most "too smart for his own good" kids.

"What is my bail? Why are they charging me with armed robbery? I didn't have a gun."

"Son, what does 'Run it' mean to you?"

"I got jacked in the hood before. I know what time it is."

"Listen, son. I'm not impressed by your sound like a brother routine. On the real? If we don't come to any agreement today on anything, let's understand one thing together, sometimes they send pampered white boys to prison too."

"Did my dad hire you?"

"No, son. The public defender asked me to help you. Your dad says you are on your own. Your mom is posting bail."

It was one of those moments in time that you never forget. The hurt in his eyes, the fear, the anger at everyone except the person who put him in this position, himself. Young boys always want to be on their own, until they are on their own.

He began, at age 15, to hang out with kids who were willing to take a few risks now and then, race cars, smoke a little weed, and maybe get drunk or high off cough syrup. The promises of tomorrow, of college, of working in "daddy's" firm just could not happen fast enough for Scott. It was fun, he thought, to get high, come home, and hide it from his dad.

I once asked him if he thought about how his dad felt about his behavior. He said he never really thought about it. But I am sure that he did. Like most young boys, he wanted his dad to discover his bad habits and to stop them. He wanted his dad to fight as hard for him as he does for his job, his clients, his image. Young boys are always trying to find a way to be men or at least be seen as a man. What they don't see, when they look at dad, is the consistency that working everyday, out of necessity, brings. So often, dad is seen as boring, distracted, "out to lunch."

Scott began to experiment with hard drugs (PCP, crack, dope, Ecstasy) when he was 17. He stole his first car for graduation. All of the guys thought it was cool.

"I had this crush on this girl named Jennie. She used to dare me to do things and I would. It would get her off when I did something crazy."

Scott lost his virginity to Jennie when he was 17.

Scott began to look for more and more ways of excitement and adventure and always it seemed that whatever he wanted to do cost money. Mom and dad had money. After all, they were professionals. Dad was an attorney for the government and a partner in a well-respected law firm. Mom was an elementary school teacher. Scott would often take cash out of their wallets or purses, but not enough to be missed (he thought). He would buy drugs, take Jennie to the movies, steal a car, and just hang out.

"Did you see yourself as a thief?"

"Not really. I guess it was just something to do and that's how I saw it."

"Taking the property of someone else is very serious."

"Yeah, I know. But I only took money, and I just really wanted to see if I could get away with it."

"Scott that's bull. You steal cars."

"I only stole the expensive cars. I figured I'd keep them a couple of days and the cops would find it somewhere when I was finished. Hell, most of these people probably have another car anyway."

"Son, did you ever stop to think what could happen if the cops ever pulled you over?"

"That happened once. I just told them that it was my mom's car and I was taking it home. They let me go without checking anything. Jennie was in the car with me and her dad is a cop."

By the time Scott reached the age of 19, he was getting high almost daily. It's easy for a young white kid to buy drugs. The quantity doesn't matter. Often, if arrested, they are charged with misdemeanors and offered every option including numerous attempts at rehabilitation. So when Scott was busted during a raid in the black community, his father's firm was able to keep his name out of the newspaper and resolve his issues separate from the seven black males arrested at the same time, all of whom faced prison terms. His record was washed so cleanly that the professors at his prestigious college thought he had missed two weeks of classes due to illness...someone else's illness. However, as many will, dad demanded an explanation and threatened to cut off funding for college if it ever happened again.

Dad and mom finally began to sense that something was terribly wrong. Jennie had entered an institution for behavior problems (it was rehab), although her parents had passed the word around that she had gone away to college. Money began to turn up missing and the amounts began to increase dramatically. They confronted Scott.

"Son, are you stealing from me?"

"Nah, dad."

"Son, are you on drugs?"

"Nah. I just miss Jennie."

"Son, if you continue down this road, you won't have a future to look forward to. Do you want to go to prison? Your mother and I work hard to put you in a position to have a solid future. If you need money, you can come to us."

Scott said he always knew these lectures were coming, but they really didn't matter. All of his friends were getting the same lectures and all of his friends were into something just like him.

"Sometimes we would go down the shore for the summer and all the parents would be telling their sons, 'Why can't you be like so and so?' I'd always laugh because 'so and so' was selling better dope or coke than you could ever get in the city and using mommy and daddy's money to cop."

It's **sentencing** day. Mom and dad are in court. They know the importance of having the court see that Scott has support and family backing. It took at least three meetings with the family to convince them that they should help. Scott had been arrested three times before and each time the father had called in favors to keep his record clean. He could not have gotten into his college with a criminal record. So on this day, Scott stood before the court with no prior convictions. However, the family was reluctant to attend and had in fact cut Scott off. They loved Scott, but they had to be tough on him, in order to help him. They didn't look so tough when they heard the facts from the judge and the victims.

Scott was scheduled to return to college following the Labor Day holiday. Rumor was that Jennie was home, so he went to their usual spots to see if she was around. She was. He was with a group of his friends and she was with her girlfriends. The two groups hit it off well. At about 11:00 p.m., he and Jennie thought that they could go off somewhere and talk, like old times. Scott didn't have a ride, neither did Jennie. So he did the next best thing. He stole a car. A white Acura.

He and Jennie drove around all night and just partied. At about 4:00 a.m., Jennie was through. She was too drunk to function and just wanted to sleep. She knew that she could not go home in that condition. Scott decided to get a room at a local hotel for the evening, but was short on cash. He drove around for about 20 minutes and decided to take a ride in the hood. He knew the neighborhood well. He and his friends would often go there to buy dope. He observed a black couple coming out of a bar. They seemed to be a little high and he thought it would be easy to get money from them. As they were getting into their car, he approached them from behind, placed his finger in the back of the gentleman and said:

"Don't move. You know what this is. Run it."

"Don't shoot," pleaded the man. "Take what you want."

Scott reached into the gentleman's pocket and took his wallet. Between the wallet and the purse, he took $225.00 and change. Jennie, who served as the lookout during the robbery, slept well that night. However, in his excitement, Scott neglected to take one extra precaution. He was followed by the victims who watched him as he pulled into the hotel, dropped Jennie off and parked the car two blocks away (in case it was recognized). It wasn't until 3:00 p.m. that afternoon that he and Jennie woke up. At about 5:00 p.m., they were confronted by the police and the victims of the crime. Scott was arrested and charged with armed robbery. Jennie was arrested too, but was released to her dad without being charged.

Theft offenses are the crimes that defense attorneys resoundingly believe are acts of desperation or stupidity. I don't know any smart thieves. Often, I wish that I could get that one case where the guy steals five million over a computer or by corporate manipulations such as, Enron or the Texas bank scandals. These criminals are usually treated as heroes and they along with their lawyers make out like bandits while their victims lose everything. He agrees to restitution knowing that the money he stole in the right interest-bearing account will make him rich when he gets off probation.

Unfortunately, I find myself representing that small-minded criminal that robs some unsuspecting, hardworking man or woman who can't afford to miss a monthly rent payment. When he "sticks" them up, the most he gets from them is $25 to $250 dollars and he puts their life and his on the line. The fear that a victim may resist, makes the thief act irrationally and if a weapon is involved, any act of resistance triggers that fear. On the street, there is nothing more frightening than a scared kid with a gun. His heart is pumping and his hands are sweating. Don't fall for this smooth, fearless criminal portrayal that is the darling of the media. Most of these kids have to get at least high to get the courage to rob and many of these acts are acts of desperation. That is why police will tell you that if someone tries to rob you, give him your property and save your life.

Then, there is the thief that breaks into your home to steal your valuables. The breaking into a dwelling with the intent to steal or commit a crime changes the title of the theft to a **burglary**. For all the planning and preparation that goes into this type of foolishness, most burglars get merchandise that they have to sell for less than half of what it is worth. After all, everyone that they are selling to knows the stuff is stolen and therefore everyone knows that the thief is in no position to bargain. Often, the person turning this thief in to the police is the person who buys the merchandise from him after the theft. He gets to keep what he wants to, if he calls it in anonymously.

My favorite thief is the **shoplifter**. Many of these thieves are women who shop at expensive clothing and jewelry stores. They know all the rules and are Oscar-worthy actresses. Unfortunately, far too many have drug problems, children they cannot feed or support, and men who do not respect them enough to discourage this conduct. Again, they steal items that they are not going to use themselves and are left to try to sell at a discount because they are in no position to bargain. Young people find shoplifting attractive and/or exciting as well. They don't understand that, as with all theft, the excitement can become an impulse or habit that will only be broken with your arrest. In the law, we call the behavior **compulsive**.

Some thieves believe that they can accomplish their goal on paper. **Credit card fraud**, **larceny**, **bad checks**, etc. all leave a paper trail. Many of these scholars will take the check or credit card to the bank or ATM machine, get their picture all over the tape and come into my office arguing that the State can't prove it was them. So what if they signed in their own handwriting? Who cares if they kept the credit card receipts in their home or car?

The silliest prosecution existing on the books these days is **welfare fraud**. Some mother who cannot afford to feed her children from the stipend given by the State and cannot find a job that pays much more than what the State is offering, decides to do both, work and accept welfare. At the end of the year when she has to report this income to the welfare board, they charge her with fraud. Get a life! Maybe, she should pay the money back by returning the extra diapers or formula she bought. Can you just see it, this mother reporting to probation along with an Enron executive or accountant, like they both committed the same offenses?

Armed robbery means that you committed a theft from a person by force or violence while armed with a deadly weapon or threatening the use of a deadly weapon. In order for the State to prove your guilt beyond a reasonable doubt, it must prove each of these elements. In Scott's case, the theft was from two persons. Therefore, he was charged with two counts of armed robbery.

Scott is right however. He did not have a weapon. So what! The presence of a weapon often doesn't matter in a prosecution for armed robbery. The fact that someone says that they have a weapon or uses something (like a hand gesture) often is enough. In our example, Scott points his finger in the back of the victim. Most jurisdictions hold that such a gesture is enough to establish the "threat" in the mind of the victim that a deadly weapon is being used. However, the belief that a weapon is being used must be reasonable under the circumstances. If the victim is credible, Scott is in big trouble.

Most armed robberies come with mandatory prison terms (5 year minimums in most jurisdictions) and are first degree offenses, meaning Scott is facing up to 20 years in prison on each count.

Such things as, a finger in a coat, a bottle, and an umbrella have all been ruled to be enough to convict a defendant of armed robbery, if it is fashioned in such a way as to make the victim believe it is a handgun. My job, in such a serious matter, is to keep this from going to trial and get Scott the deal of the century. I want to show the prosecutor, judge and, if necessary, a jury that these facts are not enough. I want to show that the facts do not support a "**reasonable belief**" that the defendant used a weapon or that the victims "reasonably believed" that a weapon was used. In seeking a deal for Scott, the discussions sounded similar to this:

"The victims didn't see a weapon and they didn't see anything shaped like a weapon."

"Come on, counsel. I have two victims and they can both identify this kid."

"Identify him as what? Someone they observed while they were drunk? Too drunk to report the crime that night. I mean, the police do say that they reported it around 3:00 p.m. How credible do you think they are going to sound when they testify, 'We didn't report the robbery that we were so in fear of because we didn't want to get arrested for drunk driving?' By the way, your male has a history, drugs, and DWI and my client doesn't. He's gonna catch hell on the witness stand and you know it."

"Will your guy plead to a second degree?"

"Make it a third degree with no recommendation. You're free to argue for jail, just give me a shot at saving this kid."

"Hell, I'm looking at his rap sheet. It looks like someone has saved him before. But it's a deal. Just let your guy know at sentencing, I'll be asking for the max."

Second degree robbery is presumably the unlawful taking by force or threat of force. Purse snatchers and bullies go to prison for this crime. A prosecutor may believe that he can't prove a weapon was used and charge the case as second degree. Second degree crimes often come with a presumption of imprisonment and in Scott's jurisdiction, a plea to second degree would guarantee his incarceration.

Give me a shot at the **third degree** and I am confident that I can keep someone like Scott out of prison. At sentencing, Scott's parents, with all of their education, professionalism, ties to the community, and "whiteness" are asked to speak on Scott's behalf. Scott's father is very reluctant (embarrassed) to come forward. This is the fourth time Scott has been involved in the court system. He has called in all the favors he is willing to call. As far as he is concerned, Scott is on his own. White people (and many "miseducated" minorities) call this "tough love." Unfortunately, he never did fight to find out what Scott was all about and fight (drop everything as Scott had hoped and needed) to straighten him out. It's not as popular as the more modern concepts, but it's been around longer; it's called "parenting." I am, however, able to convince him that he should appear and say something, if not to the court, then address Scott. He agrees.

He begins as most miseducated professionals do, and as I hoped that he would:

"Your honor. I am Scott's father. I am an attorney and Scott's mother is a teacher. I really do not know what to say at a time like this. If I may, just let me say this to Scott, you were raised better than this. You have everything going for you and you are destroying your life. I just know that this is a sad day for our family and I hope someday you get your life back on track."

Mom was even more moving. Unable to hold back her tears, she said:

"Scott is my only child. I love you son. Please get help. We will always be here for you."

You cannot plan this kind of emotion in a courtroom drama and when it comes, often it overwhelms even the hardest heart. I leaned over to whisper to Scott.

"Look at your mother. Look at the pain she's in. Is the thrill worth all of this?"

True to his word, the prosecutor argued for the max, 5 years in State prison. I argued for help for Scott and his family. He has a serious drug problem that has never been addressed and he is only convicted of **theft from a person**, a significantly lesser offense than armed robbery. He has been arrested three other times, but has never been convicted of a crime (thanks to dad's connections). He was doing B+ work in college and if he ever gets help with his drug problem, he has a bright future to look forward to.

The judge considered the arguments of all sides and I am just as sure that he considered the father's resume and dilemma. He too, was a white male and the father of a teenager . Human nature, I hoped, demanded that he consider what was best for his son. Today, Scott was his son. He is sentenced to probation (community service) and ordered to enroll in outpatient drug therapy, so that he can continue with his education.

The facts often show one clear pattern with **theft offenses**. It's a progression. If you begin by taking a quarter out of mom's handbag, knowing that you are not entitled to it, the urge to take or the thought that you are somehow justified in taking something the next time becomes easier for you to swallow. Most petty thieves do not grow up to be armed robbers, but most of the armed robbers that I know began with simple thefts and progressed.

Theft is also the kind of crime that has its own justification.

"I needed the money to pay my rent." (This armed robber panicked when the victim resisted and shot the victim in his neck. He got forty dollars along with 20 years in prison, rent free).

"I was stealing to pay for my drug habit." (This thief robbed 35 gas stations in 35 days to satisfy that habit. When the police caught him, they told him if he confessed, they could get him in a drug program. In a crack cocaine induced stupor, he confessed to 45 robberies and is doing 40 years in prison. The police closed an additional 10 cases that they could not solve).

"I just wanted to see if I could get away with it." (This shoplifter didn't get away with it. She missed her first semester at college, forfeited her tuition and eventually dropped out of college because she was sentenced to county jail time. The judge thought she needed to learn a lesson).

"**Justification**" is all that is needed for a thief to walk away with your wallet, your credit card number, your merchandise, or your life savings. When a thief has a weapon, he has usually hit a moment of desperation, a point of no return. For that moment, the weapon convinces this petty thief that he has power.

"I could see the fear in their faces. I felt it. I was in control, powerful." (This carjacker was in control for 10 seconds. The police observed the entire jack and when the scared victims got out of the car, the police surrounded it before he could get one block away. When they drew down on him with their guns in his face, he cried because he thought they were going to kill him. Imagine that. He and his mother even wondered if I could sue the police for excessive force because they "kicked his ass" after they dragged him out of the window of the car).

"I saw the coat, I wanted it, so I took it because I could." (Another "stick-up kid" who has 20 years to think about the fact that the coat he stole will be out of style when he leaves prison).

For Scott, we had stolen victory out of the jaws of defeat. For many defendants, the outcome is very different. Many defendants do not have the tacit backing of their families, families that can and do make an impression in court simply by their presence. Most criminal defendants are poor and under-represented. They don't have lawyers and teachers coming to court on their behalf. Ask most defendants if they have someone who can vouch for their good character and they only have their peers, many of whom have prior criminal records or just cannot afford to take a day off from work to come to court.

This system does not see most defendants as people with a future worth investing in. They are seen as recidivist, as extended term eligible, as career criminals, and as first offenders. The "Scotts" of the world have a clear advantage in court. His family background often gets him the additional consideration of bail pending appeal not usually given to the average defendant. His means (money) can afford him the option of long term drug treatment which most defendants cannot afford. A reasonable bail at his arrest means Scott can prepare his defense while on the street. A fifty-thousand dollar bail in Scott's world was easy, but for most defendants it's a prelude to a plea bargain because they aren't getting out of jail anyway. I was able to communicate with Scott on the street or at his home, as opposed to in the jail. The most dedicated defense attorney dislikes having to visit a client in jail and often seeks out every excuse not to. If Scott were faced with a trial, he had the means to afford experts, investigators, and character witnesses, the ability (on some level) to match the awesome power and means of the State. Most defendants cannot. People who know the system call this "white privilege."

Scott returned to college and even got a job. He told me he needed it because his parents had returned to their concept of "tough love." He laughed when he said that.

As most attorneys do, I returned to the next case. Occasionally, I would run into Scott's dad in court. He would always brag about how well Scott was doing. Two years passed since I represented Scott. One day, a young Cuban male came to the office. He needed representation.

"This kid pulls up in a car saying he wants some cracks. I go to my stash and get what he wants and he says it looks like soap. I'm like you want the shit or not? I even give him one to check out. He does. Then he puts his hand in his coat like he's reaching for his loot. He says, 'You know what this is. Run it.' I know he was strapped, I could see the handle of the gun, flat and black, and the barrel was like pointing right at my chest. ...No I couldn't see the barrel, but you know how they do. (He demonstrates). Anyway, I gave him all my money, maybe three hundred. And I gave him like six vials. He dropped the vials and that gave me a chance to pull my 9. I squeezed off a couple of shots before he pulled off. I heard the police are looking for me for assault."

I agreed to represent him. It seemed that there might be a good self-defense issue in this case and I decided to strike early by calling the prosecutor's office. I was hoping that I could turn the young man in and get the State to agree to a lower bail considering that he in fact was turning himself in and that self-defense was written all over the case.

"Hey, I'm representing a kid named X. You may have a warrant for him."

After checking her computer the assistant prosecutor responds.

"We sure do. Do you have him?"

"Well, I have access to him and I can get him in if we can agree on a bail."

"Bail? You have to be kidding. This is a murder."

I whispered to the kid that the ante and the fee just went up.

"He died huh? Well, I hear he's probably a user at worst and definitely a stick-up kid. Sounds to me like it was just a matter of time before someone took him out."

"Could be. I have his reports right in front of me. No weapon found. Three hundred-twenty dollars found on the front passenger seat. Six vials and a cell phone. Only one prior for theft."

"Was the cell phone black?"

"Yes. Why?"

"There's your weapon. And there's the self-defense."

"You're reaching counselor."

"I know, but my guy isn't a cop. He has no training or experience in this."

She laughed.

"Let me look this over a little closer and I'll get back with you. But get this guy in here."

"Fax me those reports so I know what I'm arguing against."

"They're on the way."

As I sat there reading the reports, I began to set up the argument for bail in my mind. Everything substantiated my client's version of how the shooting occurred. I was ready to turn him in and get this show on the road…until I noticed that the 22-year-old victim was a white male, named Scott.

Improbable Cause

I am not sure how the next generation is going to deal with the issue of search and seizure or civil liberties. They will probably deal with these issues with less concern or indignation than my generation and maybe lose these protections altogether. They will probably say the same things that I have heard over and over when I discuss this topic.

"I don't have a lot of sympathy for a drug dealer's rights." Or, "sometimes the end justifies the means." Or even more foreboding, "I'm willing to give up some of my rights to be protected from terrorism."

Some people have even gone so far as to posture that in a free society, you have to give up some of your rights under certain circumstances. You do not! And you better not. When you decide that some government intrusion is permissible to the detriment of your constitutional rights, you will have no liberties worth respecting. Why do you think the framers of the Constitution put in the Bill of Rights, the idea that you have the right to be free from unreasonable searches and seizures? Why do you think there is a requirement that in order for the "government" to search your home or any area you have a privacy interest in, they must first obtain a warrant and that warrant must be based on evidence of some illegal conduct? They put this right into the Constitution, along with others, because history has shown governments (no matter how well-intended) can and will abuse the power it has over people.

The government will (and did) decide that there is a correct religion in the absence of the separation of church and state. The government will (and did) decide that criticism of the government is a crime in the absence of the constitutional right to freedom of speech. The government will tell you that you cannot gather on your street corner and charge you with a crime for doing so, in the absence of the constitutional right to peaceful assembly. The government has told, and will tell you that you have no right to privacy in the absence of a constitutional right to be free from unreasonable searches and seizures. The government will (and does) violate your rights and then tells you that they are protecting the national interest. When a government is supposed to be of, for and by the people, the interest to be protected is the individual rights and liberties of the people. Rights that the framers of this democracy thought the people must have in order to be protected from the government.

Basim was a 31-year-old accountant. He was an Arab-American born in Jordan. After graduating from college, he set up shop in Manhattan, New York City. He began to develop a decent clientele with the hope and intention of making enough money to bring his father, mother, and younger brother to America. His brother was only 14-years-old and had lived along the West Bank all of his life. Basim's parents could not afford to educate the younger brother, so Basim agreed to pay the tuition at the school in the West Bank. It was the same school his parents had attended and his parents' parents. He dreamed of the day when he could afford to bring his family out of all the chaos in the West Bank to America, and to freedom.

He lived in Jersey City, New Jersey. In both New York and Jersey City, he found a large Muslim population and being Muslim, this circumstance was ideal. Eventually, he bought a house and sent for the rest of his family. He had realized the American dream and was proud to be an American. He became a citizen in 1985 and voted in his first election in 1986. Thereafter, he became a card carrying member of the Republican Party.

Basim's father was a Palestinian who had fled to Jordan during the Arab-Israeli War. Everything he owned had been taken by the Israelis following the defeat of the Arabs. He was a hard man, brought up in the old ways and traditions. He had little use for America, American customs, or an American dream. He was living the ultimate nightmare. In Palestine, he was stripped of his home, of his rights, and of his manhood without due process of law and he hated his weakness and the weakness of his people.

"They had the power, we had none," he often lamented.

After the war, he fled to Jordan with many of his countrymen. All that he had ever known about life and love was there in the Middle East. Eventually, Basim convinced him that at the age of 63, he was too old to continue hating. The concepts of freedom of speech and worship embodied in the **First Amendment to the Constitution** appealed deeply to him. He had known firsthand about government intrusion into the privacy of his home. He arrived in the U.S. in 1992.

On February 26, 1993, Basim was at his office. It was snowing that day and he was thinking about going home a little early. He asked his secretary to monitor the radio broadcasts and to keep him posted on the weather. If it was bad, he would be leaving at 1:00 p.m. and giving the rest of the staff the day off, with pay of course. It was about 12:45 p.m. or thereabouts, when "all hell broke loose."

"We didn't know if it was an earthquake or a plane crash, but we knew something was wrong."

What in fact happened was an explosion in the parking garage at the World Trade Center. Later, it was determined that a bomb had been planted there and within the time it took to say "Bill of Rights" the word was spreading that something labeled, "Moslem fundamentalists" were responsible.

"Everything changed. People who I considered friends of mine began to stay away from me. Clients began to cancel appointments. But nothing could prepare me for what was coming."

It was Friday, only three weeks since the "bombing." Basim left work early as he frequently did in order to take his father to the Mosque (Masjid) for religious services. There was an uncomfortable air about this service. As the worshippers began to gather, they noticed any number of police and FBI vehicles surrounding the entrances. One particular group of agents entered the Mosque and went directly to the Imam (religious leader).

"We have a warrant to search the premise."

"A warrant to search for what?"

"You can make this easy by opening your files and books and clearing out this place."

"What is a warrant?"

As the worshippers stood by in awe, the police and FBI ransacked the Mosque. Photos were taken of the worshippers (at random) and all the books, papers, notes, and names were boxed and taken by the FBI. Basim was stunned. Quietly, he wondered if perhaps the Imam or someone from the Mosque had been involved with the bombing, but he dared not voice that concern. He escorted his father back to the car and they returned home. On Sunday, family and friends gathered for dinner and the raid at the Mosque dominated the discussion. A rumor was circulating that the Mosque was targeted because two of the persons arrested in the bombing, were followers of the blind Sheikh Omar Abdel Rahman who had recently spoken at the Mosque.

"All of this will blow over as soon as they know that Sheikh Omar is not connected with the Mosque."

"It's not that they are targeting all Muslims or Arabs."

"You're wrong dad, America is not like the old country."

On the following Wednesday, at about 4:00 p.m., Basim was packing away his files and preparing to leave for home. His secretary approached his office. They had visitors.

"FBI! We have a warrant to search your office."

"A warrant? What is this about? I haven't done anything wrong! I want a lawyer present." Basim retorted, clearly indicating that he knew his rights.

"You're not under arrest. But then again, maybe you do need a lawyer, maybe you have something to hide," the agent countered.

Once a warrant is served, there really is not a lot of conversation about what is going to happen. The police will (should) hand you a copy of the warrant and it should outline the following:

a. The person or persons to be searched and/or seized.

b. The place, premises, to be searched.

c. The information sought by the warrant/search (e.g., drugs, papers, notes, weapons, etc.)

d. A time when the search and/or seizure can and will be conducted.

Finally, you should look to see if the warrant is signed by a judge or magistrate. If it is not, the warrant is illegal/defective, meaning you do not have to submit to the search. If it is signed, it means that the search will go on and you can challenge it later.

What is a **search warrant**? This is a document giving the government or an agent of the government the ability (right) to search you or your property. The "founding fathers" were upset with the British practice of invading the homes of the settlers, searching these homes and arresting settlers based on what they found. Maybe, they found a letter saying, "give me liberty or give me death." Maybe, they found notes saying, "taxation without representation is tyranny." A settler could be charged with treason in the 1700s for such statements. The "founding fathers" eventually felt "a man's home is his castle" and sought to make sure government was kept out of the private domain of the people.

After independence was declared, the various southern states felt that the newly found federal government had too much power and the Bill of Rights was passed to give the citizen protection from unbridle federal power. However, they understood that there may be instances when the government interest can and does override the citizen's right to privacy. Not being very trusting of "government," they therefore made it incumbent upon said government or its agent to seek and obtain a warrant before they could search a man's home or an area he maintained a privacy interest in.

What does the government need to obtain a warrant? Another good question. Simply put…"**probable cause**." Probable cause, in this context, means a reasonable belief that a crime has been committed or is about to be committed and that evidence of the crime or criminal activity associated with the crime can be found at the place to be searched. Further, the investigating agency (police, FBI) must establish to the satisfaction of a judge or magistrate that probable cause in fact exists. How is this accomplished? They begin by putting their investigation in front of the judge. This is done by having an officer testify directly or by submitting an affidavit outlining all the "facts" they believe make up probable cause. Much of the information in the investigation is hearsay (he said/she said) but it is allowed. In this case, Basim had done some accounting work for the Mosque. His name appeared on the Mosque's tax returns and payment vouchers for guest speakers. You would think more is needed in order for the government to get a warrant to invade your privacy. After all, Basim had always been a good citizen. The unfortunate problem with "good citizens" is that far too many of them believe that only criminals are subject to unreasonable searches and invasion. Only criminals have something to hide. They forget that the mere thought that the government is intruding on you, investigating you, and it can and will abuse its power, is what must be guarded against.

Obviously, the word went around the office building that the FBI was questioning Basim about the World Trade Center bombing. One office employee remembered Basim was thinking about going home at the exact time the bomb went off. He thought there was something suspicious about that and all "those Arabs" that come in and out of the office.

Basim watched in horror as the FBI rummaged through all of his files specifically removing files with Arabic names.

"This can't be happening," he thought. But it was happening. His life was being destroyed in front of his eyes and unfortunately, Basim did not see the full picture. "This type of stuff only happens to criminals," not good citizens like him, he thought. "Once they see that this is all a big mistake, I'll be back in business."

By Friday, Basim had not heard from the FBI about the return of his files. He took his father to the Mosque only to find that it had been closed. Many of the worshippers had similar experiences as Basim and were afraid to attend prayer services at this Mosque.

Basim's father understood the fear. He had seen it before. Many of the worshippers were visitors to the country and did not want to jeopardize their status or be deported. As a citizen, Basim did not have that fear. Constantly, that evening, he attempted to reassure his family that they had nothing to fear.

At approximately 5:30 p.m., Basim returned home from the office. As Basim pulled onto his street, he could see numerous vehicles and police personnel coming in and out of his home. He parked his car and ran inside.

"What the hell is going on in here?"

"Sir, are you the owner of this house?"

"Yes. Where are my parents?"

Basim was escorted (in his own home) to his father's bedroom where his father sat in handcuffs and his mother sat crying.

"What are you people doing?," he cried.

"This gentleman is a member of an organization that is on our Terrorist Watch list and is being taken in for questioning." The agent responded.

"But you can't do that. This is my home. That's my father."

"We would like to search your home."

"Do you have a warrant?"

"No, but if need be we can get one here in 10 minutes."

By now, Basim is in a panic. He had never so much as gotten a parking ticket and here he was being treated like public enemy number one; all the while his father prayed and his mother cried.

The right of privacy is fundamental to your right of citizenship. To be free from unreasonable searches of your home means that the government must state its reasons for the search and they must be reasonable under the circumstances. Should Basim let them search? Absolutely not. You gain nothing by allowing the police to search your home, especially when they have not taken the time to outline in a warrant or affidavit what it is they are looking for. If you decide to allow a search, you give up that important right of privacy.

The government has, at every opportunity, taken away pieces of your right to privacy and the "**consent search**" is one of those pieces. A **consent search** means that the party in control of the place to be searched agrees to allow the search. Consent is frequently obtained by the signing of a form, giving up your rights to resist the search. There is one critical difference between a consent search and a search with a warrant. As I explained, a search warrant must outline what it is the authorities are searching for. "We believe that the premises is being used for the packaging, sale, and distribution of narcotics."

Most courts will allow the authorities to thoroughly search for the items relative to the warrant. However, any attempt to look places where it would not be reasonable to find the items sought by the warrant would be off limits. For example, X officers are searching the premises for a shotgun. The officers begin to probe through your files. No shotgun could possibly fit there. It demonstrates that something else was on this officer's mind and often that something else is what they were searching for in the first place, but they won't admit it.

When you consent, all bets are off. The police can and will search wherever they want to. Usually, this is what happens in a motor vehicle stop, although, far too often, the search is done before the form is signed. When presented with a consent to search situation, most people believe that they have to consent. You do not. The officer will probably say, "I can get a warrant." Let him. Again, they must have probable cause in order to get a warrant and the longer he keeps you detained, the less likely it is that he can establish such probable cause. After all, if he had a reason to think you were committing a crime, you would probably already be under arrest.

Another unique aspect of the consent to search is the issue of who can consent. Drivers have been allowed to consent for the search of a vehicle even if it's not their vehicle. Parents almost universally have been given the authority to allow the search of a child's room in their home. Primarily, the issue the Court must decide when this type of a search is brought before a court is whether the child was an adult, paid rent, or held the room or area to the exclusion of the parents (in other words, told them to stay out). If there is not a lock on the door and the cops ask mom if they can search your room and she says "Yes," a court will allow anything found there to be used against you, saying you have no right of privacy.

One additional aspect of the consent search is that the person giving consent can stop that search at any time he wishes. Do not be afraid to stop it. Your stopping it cannot lead to probable cause for a warrant because you have the right to stop a consent search and they must tell you that you have this right, which is one of the reasons why they search first and have you sign later.

The twin sister of the consent search is the "**plain-view doctrine**." This legal fiction argues that if the police (in the lawful position to observe) see something illegal, they can enter your area of privacy and seize it. Typically, the police report that they received a call that some conduct worthy of investigation (criminal, suspicious) was going on at a particular residence. Knowing the person inside is not anticipating the police at his door, they knock. The person inside comes to the door and opens it. The police take that moment to scan the room or just walk in uninvited. Maybe, they see a marijuana roach in an ashtray or an empty vial. You're hit, plain view.

Did you ever wonder why, when you're pulled over for "speeding," the police officers' eyes are all over your dashboard and your back seat? They will tell you it's because they are concerned for their safety. Again, they are lying. The truth is they are hoping for a plain view sighting. Safety from a motor vehicle stop is easily obtained by asking me for my credentials, giving me my ticket, and getting out of my way.

In the criminal justice system, the State/government/police has all the power. Once it gains access to your premises, you cannot just throw the government out. Your response is to defend yourself in court with perhaps your life or reputation on the line. Unfortunately, you cannot get back the reputation you had that is destroyed by the intrusion into your privacy. You cannot recover the business you lost because you have now been associated with crime or criminal activity. Sometimes, you cannot recover from the sense of violation or the feeling that your government has taken away your sense of manhood. After all, a man's home is supposed to be his castle.

In our case, Basim's dad was detained for 18 months without a trial or due process. He eventually agreed to return back to Jordan in order to get out of detention. Basim was never connected to the World Trade Center bombing and no one knows to this day why his father was being held. His attorney was told that he was held under the principles that would eventually become the **Anti-Terrorism and Effective Death Penalty Act** passed by Congress in 1996. Under this Act, a person may be charged and held based on "secret evidence." Such evidence is to be reviewed by a judge, but does not have to be disclosed to the defendant. These defendants are being held without knowing why. In one such case, the defendant was held for two years because a disgruntled ex-girlfriend said that he had threatened the attorney general. It turned out to be bogus, but he was imprisoned without a trial or hearing anyway.

Basim lost almost everything trying to defend his father and himself. His father, having agreed to return home to Jordan, was released by the Immigration and Naturalization Service. It is rumored that he was held because an alleged "terrorist" organization known as Hamas, which was a part of the PLO was one of the organizations that sponsored the school Basim sent money to. Basim's dad continued to contribute to that school when he came to America by donating all that he had (his home, his books, and his money).

Someday, when the courts rule that locking someone up on secret evidence, violates every notion of fundamental due process and equal protections of the law that the **Fifth and Fourteenth Amendments** are supposed to guarantee, Basim's story will probably be just a footnote on the pages of this writing. It just makes you wonder if the government can and will incarcerate aliens on secret evidence (some say no evidence), whether the time is coming when citizens will face the same kind of denial of due process. Most intellectuals would have said probably not, prior to the rise to power of the

9/11 administration. But don't tell that to people like Ruben Carter, the Branch Davidians, the Move people, and an endless list of poor folks (including farmers), Japanese Americans, the American Indians' Movement, Leonard Peltier, Gary Graham, and Imam Jamil El Amin also known as H. Rap Brown, and now Arabs. They will tell you **due process**, that is the rights you have to be treated equally and fairly under the law, means nothing. When a government decides that you are the enemy, due process means nothing more than just the process that you get, whatever that is.

The new war, that is, the "War on Terrorism," is looming over the head of America and the fear factor it produces is being used by government to attack civil liberties (freedoms). The government has tried in the past to deny you this freedom; COINTELPRO being the latest exposed effort, but there have been many, many more.

The latest attacks, which are the grandsons of the House Un-American Activities Act of the McCarthy era, are the so-called Patriot Acts and the Homeland Security Acts. The "patriots" behind these acts have thrown out all of the rules on search and seizure and, through fear, have made warrant requirements and the Bill of Rights a joke. They are, therefore making America and its ideal a joke subject to their pursuit of power. If they have their way, all of the law I just described to you about search and seizure could be obsolete by the next presidential election. Get used to saying, "Hail Caesar," if you don't stop this power grab. And remember, wire taps, investigative detentions, material witness warrants, etc., are all of the things this government argued were wrong with Communism (government control of your life). Such things deter free speech, freedom to gather, freedom to travel, freedom to worship, freedom to petition—the freedoms that make this country great.

Maybe, the fear should be placed where the "founding fathers" placed it; fear of the government. God knows we have enough examples of governments willing to deny civil liberties while using misplaced fear and emotion to advance an anti-democratic agenda

(Israel, if you are a Palestinian; South Africa, if you were black; Germany, if you were a Jew; Iraq, if you were seeking freedom—the list is unfortunately endless).

The secret to recognizing governmental abuse is recognizing that we are not merely a country of laws (a concept our government is trying to imbed in our minds). We are a country of people and the government should be of the people, by the people, and for the people. This recognition argues that legislation (laws or Executive decisions) that attacks the Bill of Rights (i.e., the Right to Counsel, Free Speech, Due Process, Freedom from Unreasonable Search and Seizure, Peaceful Assembly, Religious Accommodation, Freedom of the Press, Trial by Jury, probable cause, et al.) is more destructive than any terrorist attack because terrorist may destroy buildings and perhaps many lives, but history has shown that acceptance of governmental intrusion, no matter what the motive, destroys freedom.

Judge, Jury, Executioner

Every courtroom drama has one thing in common. There is a judge; the woman or man in the black robe who instructs and guides all that occurs in the courtroom. If you elect to have a jury trial, this judge is supposed to decide the legal issues, while the jury decides the factual issues. Often, the legal issues determine how you will "try" a case and what facts are going to be presented. This person, who during the trial is supposed to be the most inconspicuous, is the one who stands out most in the mind of defense counsel. When we prepare to try a case, we have to consider the temperament of this person. We call all the lawyers we know (who have appeared before this judge) and ask all the right questions, with the hope that only one question is answered in our favor. "Will he let me try my case?"

As a defendant, you really do not know what to expect from a judge, but you are hoping that he or she will be fair. After all, everything that you have been told about this system has convinced you that in the court, you can get a fair one. You are hoping against hope. Consider the background of the person judging you or the issues surrounding your case. Their background is remarkably similar to the police officer who arrested you and who is about to testify in your pretrial motions and trial. It is similar to the prosecutor who is about to "try you" and argue that the police are credible and that you have no credibility. He or she has a vested interest in the system that is about to make you a permanent resident and has NEVER had to look at life through your looking glass.

When police officers are shown to be insensitive or disconnected from the people they are supposed to serve, sociologist and experts say it is because they see the worst in society so often that they have to disconnect in order to save their sanity. Well, imagine what it must be like for a judge who spends forty plus hours a week in the presence of criminals or people charged with criminal offenses. Every piece of research or literature they read tells them that any decision that they make could put a potential criminal back out on the streets. They judge, as most people do, based upon their very limited experiences in the real world and to protect the status quo. And because of their intellectual arrogance, they really believe they are doing the right thing.

There is this public perception that criminals manipulate the system and defense attorneys get criminals off on technicalities. That very rare occurrence is the result of some judge who realized that it is not frightening to uphold the Constitution or to seek justice. Don't expect that to happen too often. Far more often, the concept of business as usual, is the order of the day. Most judges do not want to hear what I am saying. They will argue like hell that they are fair and impartial, and judge based on the facts. You cannot convince most defense attorneys of that. Many judges are political appointees and their political persuasion is easily reflected in their decision making. Far too many are former prosecutors or public defenders and their decision making reflects the "public pretender" attitude we discussed earlier. They rule and judge as they have always believed, that you are guilty. So why are we wasting all this time? That is why most defense attorneys believe it is business as usual for judges.

The legislature has imposed certain sentencing guidelines, mandatory terms, and other rules that cut into the teeth of what a judge is supposed to stand for on the bench; the ability to be fair and impartial. Yet, the judiciary has capitulated and bowed down to these political hacks who never saw a black or poor person that they didn't think was stealing something from the "real Americans." Most judges know that many of these laws are racist in nature and application, but they are the first to sign you up for that prison bid. Unfortunately, when they do have the opportunity to exercise some discretion, like at your Miranda, Wade (identification), or suppression hearing, they inevitably decide in favor of the "status quo." You are thinking, "I can beat this" because you always think you can beat it. Well, everything and everyone involved is working against you, and the only real way out, is NOT to get in.

Barrington is a Jamaican black male. He was traveling down the New Jersey Turnpike one day with his cousin driving. The cousin is also a "homeboy." In the rear view mirrors, they could see a state trooper vehicle approximately three car lengths behind them. The driver, upon noticing this, said he made sure that he was driving within the speed limit. After following the vehicle for approximately one mile, the trooper activated his overhead lights signaling the driver to pull over. As he pulled over, the driver noticed that three other trooper cars had arrived simultaneously with the vehicle that had been following him. He knew that he had violated no laws on the road, but also knew that he had two kilos of cocaine in a false compartment in the vehicle. He had just purchased the cocaine from New York and was on his way back to Philadelphia, to do his work.

At the motion to suppress the evidence, the officer testified that he stopped the vehicle for failing to maintain a lane. According to his testimony, the trooper observed the vehicle (that Barrington was riding in) on the line leading to the shoulder of the road. After observing that, he then observed the vehicle's passenger side tires cross the line leading to the shoulder. Suspecting that the driver might be under the influence, he activated his overhead lights and pulled the vehicle over. He said he approached the driver side of the vehicle and asked the driver for his credentials. The driver was asked if he had been drinking. He replied "no." He was then asked if he would step out of the car, and he did. The trooper also noted that the driver would not make eye contact with him and appeared very nervous. He was asked where he was coming from, where he was going, and who his passenger was. He gave answers. The trooper said he then asked the passenger to get out of the vehicle, and after patting him down for his safety, asked him the same questions. After getting what he described as conflicting answers, his suspicions were aroused. He then asked the driver for permission to search the vehicle. The driver, he testified, reluctantly signed the form. It took three searches of the vehicle and the dismantling of the glove compartment to find the narcotics secreted in the vehicle. Both men were arrested.

I couldn't help but wonder, with each word of the officer's testimony, if I had been dropped off on another planet, a place where there is no Constitution. This, to me, was as clear a violation of the defendant's constitutional rights as any I had ever seen, but the prosecutor and the judge seemed to bite off of every word the trooper said, as if it were the Gospel. The more I sat there, the more frightened I became. Frightened? Yes. It was clear to me that there was no motor vehicle violation to warrant stopping the vehicle. The police cannot stop you unless there is a belief that there has been a violation of the criminal or traffic laws or unless it is done as part of their "community care taking function" (they are looking to help you). But there is not one law enforcement officer in the country that doesn't know this. So how easy is it for one of them to say, "he was speeding" or "he crossed the line to the shoulder?" These bold face lies are told EACH AND EVERY DAY in our courtrooms. Will they ever be exposed? If they are, so what!

To me, that's frightening.

"Officer, you had an initial observation that led you to believe that the driver may have been under the influence is that correct?"

"Yes."

"And you mean under the influence of alcohol, is that correct."

"Yes."

"And in your training and experience, you have learned that by speaking to the driver often you can smell alcohol emanating from him when he responds, correct?"

"Yes."

"And you didn't report anywhere that you smelled alcohol on this driver's breath or coming from the vehicle when you first approached him did you?"

"Correct."

"And that's because you in fact did not smell any alcohol at all, correct?"

"Correct."

"And before the driver was asked to exit the vehicle, there was some short conversation between the two of you regarding the credentials correct?"

"Yes."

"Now, also as part of your training and experience, you are familiar with sobriety tests, is that right?"

"Yes, I am."

"And you don't report anywhere that you gave the driver any sobriety tests, correct?"

"Correct."

"And you are taught to observe how a drunk driver walks and you listen for things like slurred speech too, right?"

"Correct."

"And you don't report any staggering or slurred speech anywhere do you?"

"That's correct."

"And that's because you didn't observe any of these things which are consistent with drunk driving or driving under the influence, correct."

"Correct."

"In fact, you don't even report that you ran his license, checked his registration or insurance, or any of the things that you would do in a routine motor vehicle stop prior to asking the driver to exit the vehicle and questioning him and the passenger, is that correct?"

"Yes."

"And I guess it was coincidental that it took four police vehicles to stop a suspected drunk driver whose credentials you never checked or who demonstrated none of the signs of DWI?"

"OBJECTION! ARGUMENTATIVE."

At this moment in the hearing, the defendant is feeling pretty good. After all, we had just shown the court that this excuse of a possible drunk driver was a pretext for a stop, or so we thought. Now, all that was needed was to show the court that the officer had the ability to fabricate, which is based on the thing that most prosecutors use to establish his credibility; that is, his education, training, and experience. Since this kind of examination of a witness is an ambush (making him think something else is happening when in fact you are going to attack it later) the officer is lured into a false sense of security.

"Officer, you testified earlier that you have been a state trooper for 10 years, is that correct?"

"Yes."

"And I assume that in that time you have made numerous traffic stops and arrests."

"That's correct."

"And during that 10 years, have you received training on how to conduct a motor vehicle stop?"

"Yes."

"And can you outline your training for the court?"

The officer then outlined the fact that he attended the state trooper academy from which he graduated. He also worked in the field under a more seasoned officer as part of his training. He attended numerous classes on motor vehicle stop procedures, search and seizure, and narcotics interdiction. He has made nearly 1,000 arrests for drugs and DWI.

"As part of your training and experience, were you taught the importance of a consent to search form?"

"Yes."

"And you were taught that if a person consents to a search, you can search wherever you want in the vehicle."

"Yes."

"And as part of your training and experience, you review the case law relating to search and seizure and consent searches, correct?"

"Yes."

"In fact, you keep a consent to search form in your vehicle, don't you?"

"Yes."

"And so when you approach this vehicle, you have all this knowledge with you. And you decide to stop the vehicle. By the way, the passenger wasn't in violation of any traffic laws was he?"

"No, he wasn't."

"So your purpose in questioning him was not because of the traffic related matter or the suspected drunk driving, correct?"

"Well, I was trying to determine if the driver was being truthful with me as to where he was coming from."

"That's another procedure that you have been taught when investigating **criminal conduct**. You question one party and then you separately question the other and if you get conflicting answers, that helps you establish that suspicious conduct is going on, correct?"

"Yes."

He thinks he said something that helps explain his actions, but what I will argue is that it really shows that he suspected criminal conduct all along. And what information did he have that would develop this suspicion?

"Isn't it a fact that all you really saw were two black males driving an out of state vehicle and for you that's enough to stop the vehicle?"

"No, you're wrong."

But I wasn't wrong. The concept is called "**Driving While Black or Brown**" or **DWB**. In the legal community, it is called "**racial profiling**" and it's illegal. Simply stated, if you are black, brown, or yellow (and I hate color descriptions of people) while traveling in many jurisdictions, in a motor vehicle, you are more likely to be stopped and have your vehicle searched than if you are white. Why? As the former head of the New Jersey State Troopers has stated and former Governor Christie Todd Whitman of New Jersey has tacitly admitted—It's a known fact that blacks and Latins sell drugs. The law enforcement community is trained to look for a black or Latin as a drug dealer or criminal. They won't deny it. But the courts do. They deny it every time they accept the word of a police officer over that of a young undereducated defendant, simply because it's a police officer testifying. The concept again demonstrates the vast hypocrisy that comes from the bench. In every trial, a judge asks jurors prior to being selected for service, if they can judge the credibility of a police officer the same as that of anyone else and not give his testimony more or less weight simply because he is a police officer. If the juror answers no, he or she is dismissed as being unable to be fair.

Imagine that you have a well-educated, trained officer testifying at a motion that is challenging his **right to search or seizure under the Fourth Amendment**. His adversary is an 18 to 20-year-old, 10th grade educated black or Latino male. The officer's education and experience allows him to understand the intricacies of search and seizure. The defendant wouldn't know a Fourth Amendment if it swallowed him whole. So, when he testifies,...

"The officer made us stand on the rail, searched the vehicle three times while the other officers guarded us. After he found the drugs, he gave us this paper to sign (a consent to search form). We didn't read it and he didn't tell us anything accept sign it and we are under arrest. The driver signed it right before they put the cuffs on us, but it was a blank form."

...Who is in the better position to lie? Is it the one who understands the law, or the one who can tell you no more than what happened to him? With little to no evidence that a crime or motor vehicle violation occurred, the Court (judge) ruled in favor of the State, concluding that the officer was credible and that the defendant had violated a traffic law establishing probable cause for the initial seizure (stop) of the vehicle. He then rules that the consent to search form, signed by the driver, gives the officer the right to search the vehicle resulting in the seizure of the drugs found in the car. In the **Dred Scott** case, the United States Supreme Court outlined the famous phrase that echoes in my heart and mind every time one of these rulings is made. "A black man has no right that a white man is bound to respect."

Defeat in a **motion to suppress** is often fatal in a criminal case. In a drug case, the fatality rate approaches 90 to 100 percent. All the drugs and paraphernalia come into evidence and it is nearly impossible to deny knowing it was in the car. Barrington didn't know. All of the evidence suggested that his driver, who was his cousin, picked him up from work at the Port Authority in New York and was giving Barrington a ride to North Jersey, before he headed to Philly. The denial of the motion also eliminates the need for a trial many times. Who's going to believe him, clearly the judge didn't. Barrington was now looking to sue for peace. The judge has now become his jury.

Oftentimes, when a defendant elects to go to trial, under these circumstances, the defense attorney will try to imply to the jury that the search and seizure of the drugs was illegal. We are hoping in this instance, that some civil libertarian on the jury (or someone who understands the importance of having a Constitution) will grasp onto this issue, as a rallying cry, to deadlock a jury we are certain has no choice but to convict if they were to simply follow the alleged facts that are presented. It's commonly referred to as **jury nullification**. Frequently, the judge will stop this kind of defense dead in its tracks.

When the judge rules that the police had probable cause to seize and/or search, they will preclude a jury from hearing any attack on the search and seizure. Many times during jury deliberations, the jurors will ask questions such as, "Did the officer read the defendant his rights" or "what if we believe the officer didn't have a reason to stop the vehicle?" The judge will tell them that issue is not in the case or, "credibility is something you can decide, but search and seizure is a legal issue not for you to decide." By the time the case gets to trial, all these legal issues are off limits to the jury.

Barrington pled guilty to a crime he said he did not commit. (Believe me it happens all the time). His plea offer was for substantially less prison time than he would have received had he gone to trial and lost. He served two years in prison, before it was discovered that the trooper (in his case) was randomly stopping motorist and "shaking them down" on the highway. The trooper had been under investigation when Barrington's case was being heard, but it wasn't disclosed. Further, after the trooper pled guilty to the shake-downs, his defense lawyer negotiated a deal on a number of DWB complaints that had been logged against he and other state troopers. He cooperated with the investigation being conducted by the State and testified that it was a routine practice for state troopers to target blacks and Latins for motor vehicle stops. Frequently, they would make up a reason to stop blacks on the highway. The consent search, he agreed, is a device they use to search for drugs or weapons because they do not have probable cause.

Barrington's case was dismissed and he was released from prison. Thirty-plus cases involving motor vehicle stops were revisited and dismissed. The trooper resigned. The judge still sits and makes these credibility calls. Usually, he makes the same call. They all do. Defense attorneys, who really understand what's happening on the streets, still fight to get these judges to understand that in the real world, some cops do lie under oath. Some cops do target certain communities. Some black, Latin, or poor people are believable. We argue on the record, and in chambers, that the courts have to stop this kind of conduct. We argue that racial profiling is real and it dominates the vast majority of cases currently in the court system, not just motor vehicle stops by state troopers. It's the way of the street, the way of the world. We argue because it's the truth and we go home with a loss. Often you don't go home.

The judges have to stand up to the legislature where race and class are more important than due process or justice. Judges have to stand up to prosecutors who have never seen fit to take the word of a defendant over a cop, even when the facts suggests strongly that the cop is lying. Judges have to stand for something in the courtroom and be seen as more than paper pushers or assistant prosecutors in order for them to be respected for their intellect, temperament, and ability. **The Separation of Powers doctrine**, of the United States Constitution, suggests that there will be three separate and distinct branches of the government. They are the legislative, executive, and the judicial. Simply stated, the legislative branch, (rich white political hacks) makes the laws. The executive branch (middle to lower working class whites, mostly male), enforces the laws. The judicial branch, (intellectual, white middle to upper class), interprets the laws. Each must have a separate and distinct function in order for the system to work properly and neither can abdicate or give up its function to another branch. Further, neither branch can usurp or take from the function of the other branches. Today, the legislative and the executive branches dominate the judicial branch, and the decisions of these courts around the country, more closely resemble the political debate surrounding the issue, than the intellectual process that demands the protection of civil liberties.

Recently, the courts have made these type of decisions:

a. Juveniles in the Washington, D.C. area can be arrested and their parents fined if they are out past 11 pm on weekdays or 12 pm on weekends.

Can someone define freedom? How about freedom of assembly? How about probable cause? All eliminated by this backwards effort at curbing juvenile crime by politicians. No one cares that most of the juvenile crime that occurs in this country occurs between the hours of 3 p.m. and 10 p.m. These are the hours that juveniles are out of school and looking for something to do. Since most of these jurisdictions, including the nation's capital, have no outlet for kids during these hours, the kids are left to find ways to entertain themselves.

b. The police, who have a reason to believe that a driver is in possession of drugs, can search a passenger without probable cause.

Talk about draconian. It is always in these decisions that the judiciary talks about how "limited" this intrusion (a search of your person by the police) is into your freedom from unreasonable searches and seizures. There's nothing limited about it. It's a disgusting, humiliating feeling. Especially, when you have done nothing wrong and especially, when you know it is really because of your skin color.

c. A grandmother who does not know that her grandson is in possession of narcotics can be evicted from public housing if the child is busted, as long as his name appears on her lease.

This law and decision was designed to stop street level drug dealing, but did anyone think that grandma or the other grandkids, that are doing well, are innocent victims? I have on my desk (as I'm writing this) the case of two Dominican boys who fell victim to this stupid law and decision. It appears that their older brother was convicted of selling narcotics three blocks away from their housing project. Housing decided to kick the rest of them out. In order to keep their mother off the street, they quit school to get jobs. One, found a job at McDonalds. The other, was too young to work, so he took up hustling. He sells cocaine now on a regular basis. At least, mom is no longer homeless. The brother who was convicted of the drug offense that got them in trouble never lived with them, but mom had him on the lease because if he ever got his life in order, she wanted to have a place for him to come. I told mom she should run for Governor of Florida or President of the United States. Then, if your kids get busted for drugs, you don't have to move out of public housing.

The judiciary must be active in its approach to interpreting the laws. It was active when it decided that "separate but equal" education (which was the law of the land) is inherently unequal. It was active when it decided that a woman has a right to choose or not to choose abortion. It was active when it decided that failure of the government to disclose potentially exculpatory evidence to the defense, is a violation of fundamental due process and the **Fifth Amendment**. Unfortunately, the level of activism that has impacted on society has come from the higher courts, and even then, only after monumental struggles. The courts that deal with the day-to-day criminal process are missing in action.

The legislature, on the other hand, has always been actively resistant to the legitimate concerns surrounding civil liberties and is consistent in pursuing its anti-minority, anti-poor agenda. The executive branch, which includes the police and prosecutors, is often viewed as the occupying army in minority communities and operate hand-in-hand with the legislative agenda. Both attack the constitutional liberties of minorities and poor people every opportunity that they get under the guise of being tough on crime.

Regrettably, the judiciary will not respond to any call for help. They could stop racial profiling overnight. They could check **police brutality** (that is, the use of excessive force) at the door. They won't. So the next time you see a defendant assert his innocence, watch the bench closely as they wheel that defendant off to prison on the weakest of evidence. In Barrington's case, the judge was black, but it was still business as usual. That gave Barrington some concern.

"Do you think that he just didn't believe me or that he didn't believe me because I'm black?"

"I can't answer that for you. Let me say, that I've been involved in stronger cases that have been ruled the same as yours and weaker cases that we won. But wouldn't it be something if he didn't believe you because HE is a black man?"

"Well I thought the brother would give us a fair hearing. I was wrong."

"I'm certain that most of these judges don't have a frame of reference for judging the credibility of brothers like you. And I'm just as certain that they don't use the frame of reference that they have for judging police. So either way, black or white they sell the profession short."

I explained to Barrington when a judge is on the bench, the only semblance of "blackness" you will see is in the robe he wears. Many of my colleagues tell me that is the way it should be. I can't help but disagree. Just once, I'd like to hear a judge (any judge) say, "I'm from that hood and the brothers don't roll like that." Or, "I've heard this story before, this guy lies every time he comes into my court." A few more Honorable Bruce Wright's would do the bench and the discussion of criminal justice a huge favor. Instead, what I get from the bench is arguments about why it's taking so long to plead the defendant out or the judge asking more questions at trial than the prosecutor.

At the end of the day, the real question is what do these judges see when they see you in court? The answer far too often is someone who's culture, class, and lifestyle they have no frame of reference for. Except, that most of the black or poor people they come in contact with, are guilty of a crime.

One Good Cop

In the criminal justice system's pursuit of the "truth," there is this misguided, but conscious propaganda that attacks people who criticize police officers or police conduct. They argue that those who criticize the police are doing the country a disservice. They argue that criticism of the police will eventually lead to police being hesitant when confronting crime for fear of the criticism. It is a specious, disingenuous, often simply ignorant, argument. How often do you hear, you cannot make generalities, you can't say all cops are bad because of the conduct of a few? Stop! We say that all the time about young black males, about lawyers, about athletes, about poor white mothers on welfare, and no one complains. Of course, it is a generality. But there is a greater point. The people who work everyday with the bad apples have to discard those bad apples. If they do not, who will? If they do not, then they suffer from the bad stench these people bring to their profession. It's like that in every walk of life. Heaven only knows how many times I have been called an "ambulance chaser" because some lawyers do that. Imagine if one officer had taken the initiative to cover Rodney King from the beating he was taking. Imagine if one officer had shown some restraint or compassion for Ahmed Amadou Diallo in New York (41 bullets fired)—Tasha Mayes in New Jersey (36 bullets fired into a van)—Johnny Gammage in Pittsburgh (beaten to death by police during a traffic stop), or Archie Elliot in Maryland (shot while handcuffed following a motor vehicle stop).

In Chicago, two boys, ages 8 and 9, were charged in the brutal rape and murder of a 12-year-old girl. She was sexually assaulted and her panties stuffed in her mouth according to reports. The two boys apparently were "maneuvered" into confessing to the crime, although why anyone would take a confession by an 8-year-old seriously is mind-boggling. Eventually, someone had an inspirational thought similar to the one held by my eldest daughter. Semen was found in the dead girl and my then 14-year-old daughter (along with that crack investigative team in Chi-town) wondered if an 8-year-old boy could produce a semen sample. Common sense demanded that this case be dismissed, and eventually it was. However, one good cop stepping forward in that matter, could have stopped the absolute trauma and fright that these boys will endure for the rest of their lives. But far too often, being a "good cop" means something different to cops than it does to ordinary citizens.

It was a midsummer's night in the city. David and Jessica were just returning home from the Puerto Rican day parade. David, like so many minorities do, celebrated with a 40 oz. and had gotten a little high. They had gotten home at about 8 p.m. and since it was sweltering, David thought he would chill a bit on the front porch. He loved Jessica and she loved him. At about 9 p.m., he was feeling "kinda nice." A car pulled up and in it was Jose, his boy.

"Qué pasa bro?"

"Chillin."

"Yo Poppi, that parade was the shit, no?"

"You know what I'm saying."

"Yo, we going down by the river meeting some people down there, party a little. You down?"

"Yeah I'm wit' it. Let me holla at Jess."

He leans into the front door and yells that he is going with Jose and will be back by midnight. He's gone. Jessica was in the shower and didn't hear him. They had a 5-year-old son together. His name is Raul. Raul was supposed to be asleep, but woke up when David yelled into the house. He went to the front door. David never locked it, after all it was hot and they had no air conditioning. The screen door was as much air as they could hope for. Raul left the house looking for his "poppi." When Jessie finished her shower, she checked the baby's room to see if everything was fine. The baby was gone. She didn't panic, there was no need. Maybe, the baby was on the porch with David. She went to the front door. No David and no Raul.

"They must be together," she thought.

She turned on the television and waited. At ten o'clock she checked outside again. No one was there. She began to worry.

"I'll call David on his pager. He always keeps it on him and he usually calls me right back," she thought.

David got the page, but he was on the waterfront and just assumed that it was nothing important. He would call as soon as he could get to a telephone. At about 10:30 p.m., Jessica called David's pager again.

"Yo, homes, you better check in."

"Yeah Dave, we don't want Jess kickin' your ass again."

The fellas got a good laugh out of David that night. But this time David went and found a telephone.

"Hello. David."

"Yeah it's me. What's up?"

"Where are you? Why you got the baby out so late?"

"What? I don't have the baby."

"Oh shit! You better be playing."

"I'm not playing."

Jessica began to feel the overwhelming sense of fear that only a mother can explain. As the tears swelled up in her eyes, her mind raced back and forth to all of the worst scenarios. She began to shake and cry and scream.

"David, the baby's not here, he's gone! I thought he was with you!"

"Call the cops. I'm on my way home."

David and the fellas immediately jumped into the car and headed for home. Normally, it is about twenty minutes away. Tonight, it would be different. The vehicle traveled (often) in excess of the 35 mph posted speed limit and soon it was pulled over by the police. Two officers were in the patrol unit and there were five Latino males in David's vehicle. The officers approached with caution. They testified that they could see a lot of movement inside of the vehicle and it aroused their suspicions. The front seat passenger seemed particularly to be moving about a lot. Finally, David, the front seat passenger, attempted to exit the vehicle. He felt the officers would understand, if he just explained. He exited the vehicle quickly and the officers responded by drawing their weapons.

"Get back in the car. Get back in the car NOW!"

"Look officer..."

"Get back in the car."

The fellas yelled to David to get back in. By this time, the officers had retreated to their vehicle to call for back up. The broadcast stated "We have a potential incident, officers need assistance, urgent. Five black or Hispanic males may be armed."

David got back in the car. The wait was killing him. He was only five minutes away from his home, his girl, and the search for the baby. Four patrol units arrived on the scene (three from the middle shift that would usually sign off at 11:00 p.m.). One unit arrived from the midnight shift that was just signing on. In all, there were now five police units with six police officers on the scene. The vehicle was surrounded and each of the passengers was "pulled" from the car, one at a time. David was "pulled out" by the officer from the midnight shift.

"Look we were speeding, but my kid is lost, I'm just trying to get home."

"Shut the fuck up!" yelled the first officer, who had stopped the vehicle.

"Man, you guys are wasting time. I gotta get home."

Another officer, hearing that comment, smacked David in the back of his head. David, the midnight officer would testify, seemed distracted. For ten minutes, they all stood on the curb while the original officers searched the stopped vehicle. In the back seat, under the cushion, he found a small bag of marijuana.

"I got something here. Lock their asses up."

"Lock up who? I'm going home," David responded.

"Especially the big mouth, you going to jail papi."

David could only think of Raul. Jail was not a consideration. He broke and ran heading for home. The original officers drew their weapons intent on firing, but the midnight officer stepped in.

"He's not armed. Catch him."

The officers chased David. The 40 oz. he had been drinking began to catch up with him too and he began to vomit and stagger. He fell and the officers pounced on him. Each time he tried to get up, they would hit him with their batons. He could only think of finding Raul. They beat him and beat him, but he would not stay down. Finally, the other officers arrived at the scene (with David's friends) in their police vehicles. Again, the midnight officer intervened.

"That's enough. Get to your feet, if you can son. He's coming with me."

Twice during the beat down, David tried to raise himself up by grabbing onto the police officer. When he woke up the next morning, he was in the local hospital. He had been charged with aggravated assault on a police officer, attempted possession of a weapon, resisting arrest, as well as, possession of marijuana. He received 37 stitches to his head, 10 stitches above his right eye and he lost two teeth. When he eventually came to, he had no idea where he was.

"Where's Raul?" was all he was heard to mumble. He cried a lot. Jessica was at his bedside. She cried too. Raul had not yet been found. When David heard this, he tried to get up, but between the pain and the medication, he could not move. Jessica explained that she had contacted the police, but there was no word on Raul. They cried together. His family arrived at the hospital, but could not visit him because he was a prisoner, as well as, a patient. They prayed and cried some more.

At approximately 8:00 that evening, there was a knock at his hospital door. The police…and Raul. He was safe. Jessica hugged him as if she would never let him out of her arms again. David thanked God. He could not muster up the nerve or courage to thank the police. He couldn't even see his son since both of his eyes were swollen shut from the beating. He hated cops. He had been done wrong and wanted no part of any cop.

After assuring David that Raul was healthy and fine, Jessica left with the police to fill out some paperwork. She was left with mixed emotions. The police had beaten her husband nearly to death, but had also saved her son. Still she and her family wanted to thank the officer who found the baby. They went down to the precinct to meet him. He had called in sick and would not be back until the next evening's midnight shift. They came back the next day to meet him. When the officer arrived at the precinct, he was met by reporters, news crews, and his superiors. He was a hero, he had saved a life. He was the best of what the police had to offer. Jessica and her family had baked him a cake, some small token of their enormous appreciation. He did not like the attention from the media for doing his job. The saving of Raul and the meeting with family members made the newspapers as did David's arrest. The beating of David did not. Privately, the officer talked with the family.

"Where did you find him?"

"He was at the Arcade on Main Street."

"Oh my god, that's two miles away. How did you know to look there?"

"I saw a picture of him in your husband's wallet. In the background, was the arcade. Children who are lost usually go someplace familiar or someplace fun. So I took a chance that he might be there."

"How did you get David's wallet?"

"I was out there when he was arrested."

Nothing can really prepare you for what it is like to be a defense attorney. All the emotions, all the stories, all the fears, all the hopes are placed in your hands. Your skill is put to the test each day. Your compassion is tested each day. Your sense of right and wrong is challenged by every case, every statement, every cop, every prosecutor, and every client. David spent three weeks in the hospital recovering from his injuries before he was taken to jail. He spent another six weeks in jail before he could make bail on the charges that now had been upgraded to attempted murder of a police officer. David and I had been friends for a long time. He was good people. A little hot-headed, but hard working. Jessica contacted me while he was in the hospital and I reluctantly agreed to represent him.

When you sign on to represent family and friends in a criminal matter, it is hard to remain detached. If you lose, you are no longer arguing for some stranger that you know only by a receipt book. You are arguing to save someone you love or respect and for many attorneys, it's too much to handle.

After a year and six months, the matter was called to trial. I had pursued a dismissal of this matter at every turn, but the State was confident in its ability to prove its case against David and the only plea offers were for State prison bids. David rejected all offers, short of an apology from the police. At trial, the prosecutor called three of the police officers as witnesses. They all testified that after the marijuana was found, David broke away and ran. The State argued that running, shows a **consciousness of guilt** (he ran because he committed a crime and was trying to get away). They gave chase and caught David when he fell. Their intention was to place him under arrest and he was told that he was under arrest. David, they continued, refused to submit to the arrest, forcing them to use the reasonable force necessary to subdue him. During his resisting, he twice attempted to grab the police officer's handgun, which forced them to use their batons repeatedly to stop him from gaining the advantage.

"If we had not used the batons the way we did, he would have gotten hold of the gun and used it."

Obviously, that testimony was objectionable, but the absurdity of it, I hoped would be seen by the jury. I did not object, but after allowing the testimony without objection, I began to question that strategy. I had one ace I still had to play. I called, as my only witness (other than David), the midnight shift patrol officer. He was subpoenaed one day before he was supposed to testify and had no idea why he was testifying. I timed it that way. When he was entering the courtroom, I could see him meeting with the other officers who had testified. They all had submitted reports, but he had not. They all had met with the prosecutor and each other and had gone over their testimony in preparation for trial. He had not. They all seemed genuinely surprised that he was being called at all, which was exactly what I had hoped for. As I watched them talk in the hallway, I wondered if they were sharing their story with him, if he would go along with the company line.

My instinct for calling him was based on the fact that he had stopped the others from firing on David that night and had stopped the beating. He was the one who had searched the entire night and, when his shift ended at 8 a.m., he stayed on the street, on his own time, and searched until he found the baby.

Once, when I was a kid, I was busted for shoplifting. The police officer that caught me, Officer Moe Jenkins, should have and could have arrested me. He didn't. He told me how tough it would be for me, if I had a criminal record, to get into college or make something positive out of my life. He also took me to the police station to show me what jail looked like and told me if I got involved with stealing, that this would be my home someday. Then, he took me home and told my parents that I was a good kid. He said that I was interested in police work, so he drove me around. He covered my butt, literally. I owe him. I saw, in both these officers, a concern, for the people they were sworn to protect and serve. On both occasions, I was right.

In law school, you are taught to never ask a question you do not know the answer to. In this instance, I believed I knew the answers and was sure that he had the character I could trust to tell the truth.

"Officer, I call your attention to the date in question. Were you present when the vehicle was searched?"

"Yes."

"Please tell the jury what, if anything, happened there."

"When I arrived, the vehicle was parked. I could see there were five males in the vehicle and the six of us surrounded it. I removed the passenger who told us he was trying to get home because his baby was missing."

"Who said that?"

"The gentleman at the table." (Identifying the defendant, David). "He seemed so distracted. I had heard the broadcast that a child was missing, so I assumed he was being truthful. When the marijuana was found, he said something like, 'I'm not getting locked up. I've gotta go home.'"

"What, if anything, happened next?"

"He ran. The others were secured while three officers gave chase."

"Did any of these officers draw their weapon and point it at David?"

"Yes. They all did. But that was precautionary. When a suspect breaks and runs like that, you never know if he's going to draw a weapon or if one of the others had a weapon. But since, I had searched him, I knew he wasn't armed."

Since, I am usually the one cross-examining police officers, I therefore limit their answers to a series of "yes/no" responses. This time, however, I had to let the officer talk more. My hope was that he would contradict the others and that he would be credible. It is like an unwritten law, in many predominately white jurisdictions, that you do not call a police officer a liar. Most jurisdictions with western educated people, with Euro-centered education, trust the police. In jurisdictions where the education or experience is not western or status quo oriented, they trust the police less and expect them to lie. Without this officer, it's David's word against the police, frequently a losing proposition.

"Did you observe the officers when they caught up to David?"

"Yes."

"Please tell the court what, if anything, you observed."

"The officers chased the defendant for about 200 feet before he fell. It looked like he was staggering and I assumed that he had been drinking. The officers immediately jumped on him and attempted to place him under arrest."

David looked at me. He was upset with my decision to call this officer. All we had going was my instinct.

"All of these cops are alike," he thought. "He's going to lie just like the rest."

I continued with my questioning.

"Officer, when you say, they 'jumped on him', what do you mean?"

The officer hesitated as if searching for just the right words to complete his thought.

"The defendant had fallen and when he attempted to get up, one of the officers struck him in the back of his head with his baton. Each time the defendant attempted to get up, he was struck. I stepped in because I thought I could stop the beating and make the arrest."

I paused, hesitated, almost afraid to ask the next question. Still, when you have tried enough cases, you understand that a pause can enable the jury to "soak it all in," and they don't ever have to know that you are nervous as hell.

"Did you observe the entire chase and catch?"

"Yes."

"Did you lose sight of the defendant or the other officers while you were guarding the other gentlemen?"

"No. I didn't guard the others. When the defendant ran and the other officers began the chase, I got into my patrol unit and pursued. I could see them all because I parked my vehicle in the direction they ran and they really didn't run that far before the defendant fell."

By now, I was confident that this officer was going to tell the truth, the whole truth, and nothing but the truth. The next series of questions were the "questions" I should never ask because I didn't know the answer. But I let it fly anyway believing in my client's story, which up until now, had matched much of what this officer was testifying to.

"Did you ever see the defendant in possession of any weapon prior to the chase?"

"No."

"Did you ever report anywhere that you saw him grab for a weapon at any time?"

"No."

"Usually, when you observe that kind of conduct from a suspect, possessing a weapon or grabbing for a weapon, is that something you would regularly make a note of?"

"Yes."

"And you never reported any conduct of that nature from the defendant, correct?"

"Correct."

"Is that because while you were observing this chase and arrest from start to finish, you never saw this defendant grab for any officers' weapon?"

"Objection!"

"Counsel this is your witness and the question is leading. Objection, sustained."

Objection sustained means that the judge agrees with the person objecting (that the question was improper or phrased improperly). This kind of examination was necessary because I did not know how the officer would answer the most critical question in the case. Strategically, I asked the leading question with the hope that I would get an answer before the objection, and I did. While the prosecutor rose to his feet to object, I focused on the officer's mouth, his eyes, his body language; for some sign that the answer was NO. I read him right.

"I'll rephrase it judge. Officer, tell this jury why you didn't report seeing any conduct such as the defendant grabbing for an officer's service weapon."

"Because he didn't grab for one. He was being beaten badly and kept trying to get up. Twice, he reached for the nearest person to pull up on, but it was clear, that all he was trying to do, was to get up. One officer even commented that he almost pulled his pants down."

That was the answer I was hoping for. I was now confident in getting this officer to describe what "badly" means, how many times the defendant was struck and that he called for emergency medical assistance because of the severity of the beating.

"Did you stop the beatings?"

"Not immediately. I was calling the arrest in and when I finished, I stepped in. The defendant grabbed my belt area in order to pull himself up. He was pretty well beaten. I should have stepped in sooner, but I didn't."

The jury was out deliberating the case for nearly two days. That wait is often unbearable when (literally) someone's life is on the line. You cannot console or comfort the defendant who wants to know if a quick verdict or a long deliberation is better for him. "You can never tell what a jury is thinking Dave." You can't really work because your mind is retrying your every move during trial. "Did I miss something? Should I have let that testimony in? Why did I ask that question? What happens if they find him guilty? Who will take care of Raul and Jess?" You pace and think. You sweat it out, just like the defendant, trying to convince yourself that it is only business. But if you ever resolve that it is "only business" (a lot of us do) you sold out the life that's in your hands.

Finally, a verdict. Not guilty, on all counts. I wanted to celebrate, but when I looked to my left, David just sat there crying. Often, as defense attorneys, we forget the fear and anguish that this process can put a person through. Often, we are on to the next case or counting our money or victories (never our losses) so quickly that we forget that the client is a person. For him, this was a matter of life and death. The system saw him as a criminal. The court saw him as a case. The defense saw him as a strategy. David went to trial to prove he was a man worthy of belief. He put his life in my hands and reluctantly trusted my instincts. We won. And for one moment, looking at David cry, I reclaimed a sense of my own humanity. David's tears became my tears. We cried together.

It had been three years since David's trial. One day, while I was waiting in Newark, New Jersey at the train station for a train to Washington, D.C., someone called out to me. I turned and saw a uniformed officer. Since, I did not recognize the uniform, I did not recognize the face.

"Remember me?"

"Sorry officer, No, I don't."

"Remember that trial? I found the little baby boy."

"Oh, definitely. How are you? Hey, that's a different uniform, are you moonlighting?"

"No. That's a long story."

The officer and I talked about what it was like for him at the police division that he had formerly been working with. He said that I was the only defense attorney to ever call him as a defense witness. Basically, it made him look like a "rat" to the cops in his division. The word went around that he could not be trusted and thereafter no one wanted to be partners with him. Regularly, on calls, he felt that he could not get any backup or support, except from the younger officers with little to no experience. He tried to become a detective, but was headed off at every turn in the department. He volunteered for a couple of undercover assignments, but was often left with no backup. He related that on one assignment, he was fired on and no one came to his aid. He felt that had he stayed in his former position, he would either get killed, or kill himself. He began to drink heavily and sought counseling for depression because of this treatment by fellow officers. He left that police department, taking a less prestigious position, but still one where he could protect and serve, which is all he ever really wanted to do.

Cops, he confessed, have a code. It is an unwritten code, but it's a code of fraternity that many interpret as covering a fellow officer's back. When one officer turns another in or testifies against other officers, he's considered to have violated the code and therefore cannot be trusted. We argued and debated the issue of whether the police can "police the police." Frankly, if they are corrupt, there is no one to check them. Only when something major happens does the real conduct of what is going on in the streets come out. In Los Angeles, a Sheriff's officer was busted because four to six pounds of cocaine turned up missing in one of his cases. He has since "ate cheese" on a number of officers, resulting in the reconsideration of numerous cases where they allegedly fabricated evidence, shot innocent citizens without cause, had witnesses to their crimes deported, and lied on the witness stand while under oath. Absent the mistake by this public servant, no one would give a damn that they have these kind of cops in LA. But I'm telling you this is the norm in these street crime and narcotics units throughout the country. We argued.

"But what about what's right and wrong? How do you live with that code when you know a cop is outright wrong?"

"That's something you keep in the family. Something you work out with that officer. Honestly, if I had known why you were calling me in advance, I may have testified differently. I don't know that I would have, but I might have."

"I respect that, but the truth has to be bigger than our codes and friendships, don't you think? After all, people are going to jail everyday behind cops keeping shit in the family."

"That's easy to say. But I lost a lot of friends and left the job I loved. I don't know."

"You saved three lives. One life at least twice. You were the kind of cop I grew up respecting and that the community wants to see and deserves. Frankly, you may not have the job, but these punks they have out there doing the 'job', have zero respect and no integrity. This criminal justice thing is tough and it seems that nobody is interested in just doing the job right, because it's the right thing to do."

"Counselor, you sound like my wife and kids. But how can someone like me, who wants to do right, help if I am not on the force? If I turn in cops who change a fact or two in a report, I'm a traitor. If I do that and some criminal goes free, how do you think I'm gonna feel? I lose my job and then I have nothing."

"Come on. You and I both know that some of these guys are lazy and bad for the profession. They need to be turned in. I'm serious. Cops take the witness stand daily knowing that people are going to believe them because they are cops. They lie knowing that even if they are caught in a lie, there is no fall out. And what's worst, none of you (cops) are turning in other cops. Compared to all the lies they tell in the courts, and the lives they are destroying in the process, how can you say with a straight face that cops turn cops in? When they get caught in a lie, they go back to their precinct and talk about how they were tricked by the defense attorney."

"I'll remember that, the next time you call me as a witness."

We laughed, but we both recognized the seriousness of my accusation. Conduct that would be considered criminal in the eyes of a "good cop," if it were you or I committing it, is however, overlooked by that same "good cop" when another police officer is involved. The officer who complains or reports other officer's criminal conduct is often the one who is disciplined for insubordination, so why do it? Even more compelling in the eyes of the criminal justice system is the fact that the police and the courts recognize and understand this concept of a double standard for police conduct or misconduct.

Ordinary citizen Joe Jones shoots an unarmed man because he thought the man had a gun or was reaching for a weapon. Joe Jones will face a murder charge with literally his own life on the line. Officer Doright, who shoots and kills an unarmed man because he thinks he is reaching for a weapon, may face criminally negligent homicide at best (with the prospect of probation if convicted) and in most instances will never even get indicted.

The Phillip Pennells, Anthony Biases, and Prince Joneses of the world will never see justice and EVERY officer who has ever fired his weapon knows this. This is why they are so shocked and dismayed when one of their "brethren" is indicted on even the most obvious crimes. Further, they know that no prosecutor can prove criminally negligent homicide to the satisfaction of a judge, so they regularly select a non-jury trial. Also, they know that since these crimes are being investigated by their brethren, not even a good prosecutor can control how the brothers in blue subtly destroy the government's case by a lack of investigation or by constant failures of recollection while testifying.

I asked him if he told the truth on the witness stand. He paused, and said yes, he had. I told him that I called him as a witness because the facts showed that he was the one thing I respected in this entire process, a good cop. As I boarded my train, he called out to me.

"Hey, chief. You know I heard from your client about a year ago."

"Really? You know he hates cops."

"Yeah, he sent me a picture of him and his family. Well, it probably was from his wife. On the card it said, 'Thank you'."

"Looks like you made a believer out of someone else…" I said laughing. "Who knows, little Raul may grow up and be a cop because of you…or even better… a defense attorney."

Each time I cross-examine a cop or just have idle, friendly conversation with one, I wonder out loud if they really understand the job. I don't want police in my neighborhood that believe it is proper or acceptable to walk up to me and ask me who I am or where I am going. I don't care what the law says about reasonable suspicion or stop frisk. I want what I always want when I am in the projects or on Main Street, or in court; RESPECT. Don't tell me that I live in a high crime area when 85% of the people arrested in my neighborhood are arrested for drug-related offenses and 75% of all of those in rehab or using narcotics, are from another community. The reality doesn't support the argument that my community is high crime. Every two minutes, a woman is raped in this country. Who's raping all these women? Blacks make up less than 18 percent of the population; Latinos about the same. Considering that most crime is committed by persons of their own community (black on black, white on white, Latino on Latino) it seems that a lot of rape is being committed that is not being reflected in the political and media face that is being put on crime. I recently read that a burglary is committed every 14 seconds. I just cannot see all these black and Latin burglars running in and out of white communities like they are running in and out of the jails.

In my community, two boys get into a fight and they are both subject to criminal prosecution. In some communities, they get into a fight and the local officer scares them (with a potential arrest) and takes them home. That's policing. Policing is a community function. If you have no "sense of community," get a job in the community you do have a sense of service and respect for. But get the hell out of mine! In one case in Virginia, I watched as four African-American juveniles were arrested. They were charged, pleaded guilty, and placed on probation while the one white boy in the same car with them, involved in the same activity, was arrested, allowed to call his parents, sent home and eventually had his case dismissed. That's one statistic in the black community that says "crime" and another statistic in the white community that says nothing.

The police see you a certain way and you, potential victim of the police, must come to an understanding of how they perceive you. When this officer, who was a good cop, said, "...if I do, and some criminal goes free..." I thought, "if you just think about what a criminal looks like, the face of crime in America is black, brown, and/or poor." So if that face is dignified looking, white, shirt and tie, educated, he can almost get away with murder. Names like John List, Nicholas Bissell, Susan Smith, Jeffrey Dahlmer, Amy Grossberg, Brian Peterson, N.Y. City Street Crimes unit, come to mind. Maybe, that's why Gotti stayed so dapper for so long.

In court one day, a colleague approached me and asked me if I knew this "good cop." He was wondering if I would be a character witness for him.

"Witness? Why? Is he in trouble?"

"Oh, no. He is thinking about suing the police department he used to work for."

It appears that after he testified in our case, he had in fact reported misconduct by the other officers. He had observed officers associating with drug dealers, using narcotics, using unnecessary and excessive force on civilians, illegal searches, and fabricating, or planting evidence on innocent people. When his superiors heard his stories, they told him to keep them to himself. He then, knowing that he had literally placed his life on the line, and knowing that he could get no support from his own people, sought the advice of legal counsel, psychological counseling for depression and, eventually, the position with another law enforcement agency.

I laughed. I finally understood that he was "playing me" during our chat. He believed in the profession and was just feeling me out, seeing if I was a true believer, I thought to myself (with a smile),

"David was right. He was a liar after all just like the rest of them."

I agreed to be a witness on his behalf (if he ever decided to sue). After all, I knew from experience, that if he was going to be taking on the police, he was going to need all the help he could get. Rumor has it that he kept a diary on police abuses that could have exposed any number of officers to discipline and possible criminal charges. Rumor further has it that he intended to expose these abuses. I never did testify on his behalf.

The last I heard was that he gave up on the profession, gave up on the lawsuit, and gave up on life. He killed himself. One bullet to the temple in his living room.

But you know what the rumor is don't you?

Pleas, Please, Pleas Please

After all that I've already told you, you may still think that when you get involved in the criminal justice system, you can get a fair one. You may still think that you can get some justice in the court. Well, you can if you define justice as **"due process."** What is due process? Simply stated, it is whatever process is due to you. You can and will always get that (or something similar) and at the end of the day when you are wondering what just hit you, someone will tell you that it's the best deal in town.

Most of the persons who enter the criminal justice system resolve their matters by way of **plea bargain**. The matters are resolved that way for any number of reasons. Obviously, the most common reason is "I did it. Can you get me a good deal?" The general public hears this and thinks that you just got away with murder. They are wrong of course. They are caught up in the publicity that comes with crime and punishment in this country. They are listening to the politicians and media who have a vested interest in scaring people about criminal conduct and who cannot believe that these "criminals" are not in jail for life. When a person gets the benefit of the plea bargain, it's almost always because the process functions better this way. Imagine what it would be like if everyone involved in the criminal justice system were forced to go to trial. The system would grind to an immediate halt and it would cost taxpayers a fortune that they are not willing to pay. (Which, frankly is the reason why the legislators push these mandatory terms and ridiculously harsh penalties. They don't want people challenging their cases in court, they want them facing penalties at trial that would make them plea if something reasonable is offered).

Pleas help the process. Incidentally (and on rare occasions) they help the defendant. Some of the considerations that go into a plea bargain may help you understand what the system is really about.

John was a 21-year-old, third-year college student. He had no prior involvement in the criminal justice system. He was asked by his cousin, a drug dealer, to carry a bag for him. The cousin, who knew it was "hot" on the street (meaning the police are all over the area) was serving John up like a happy meal. John got busted. The police stopped him and asked if they could search his bag. He hadn't done anything wrong, so he consented. Never consent! If he were busted by the "feds," the amount of drugs in the bag would have had John facing life imprisonment. In this case, he was lucky, I guess. He was busted by local detectives. In the state he was busted in, the maximum prison term for this crime is 20 years. He was charged with a first degree crime, but because of his lack of prior involvement, the plea offer was to a lesser, second degree, weight (meaning the maximum he was facing was 10 years, if he took the plea).

"But Mr. Bashir, I didn't do anything."

"I believe you. But what do you think a jury is going to believe, if you go to trial? The detectives will testify that they had a tip that there would be a person carrying a green bag who was delivering crack. They saw you and the bag and asked you to consent to a search. You did. You gave up any search and seizure issue you might have by signing the consent. And they don't have to lie to prove you had it in your possession."

"Don't you have to know something is there to possess it?" he asked.

"Yes." I responded. "In fact, you have to know what it is, where it is, and the nature of it. Just understand that if you elect to go to trial, it's going to be your word alone. Please think this through. I'm not saying you can't win, but you better be damn sure you want to take this shot. I'm pretty sure I can get your offer down to 7 years, you'll probably do 2. That's a lot better than the 15 you'd get with a mandatory 5, if you lose."

"Bash, I can't do two minutes in jail."

On the prosecution side I hear:

"Mr. Bashir, I can't go lower than second degree."

"Come on. This guy has nothing in his background. No juvenile history. No adult history. He's a college student. He just has a cousin who we both know is in the game. Don't hurt this kid like this."

"I've got a case I can prove and only his word that he was not involved. You don't seriously expect me to dismiss against him."

"Seriously? Yeah, I do. Or give the kid the benefit of the doubt somewhere."

"If he can get his cousin to admit to it, I'll consider letting him out."

"You know that's not going to happen."

"It could, if your client is willing to work."

"You mean set the cousin up?"

"That and help in other ways. Like maybe become an informant. We could keep him confidential."

"I'm telling you he is not in the game like that. He wouldn't be believable. And he could end up dead."

"That's the best I can offer."

John refused the plea bargain and refused to become an informant. He also refused to believe that his cousin set him up. He went to trial and lost.

John was sentenced to 15 years in prison, 5 years without parole. Since he had no prior involvement, he qualified for an early release program and was back on the streets at the age of 24. Jobless, on parole, angry, and labeled as a drug dealer, he felt his life was ruined, so he took up dealing drugs with his cousin. One day, his cousin told him not to be on the block because it was "hot." In the meantime, he watched as his cousin, who had never been busted, called one of his runners and asked him to deliver a package somewhere. The runner (some kid called DC) got busted and was later sent to prison.

John began to see the real world clearly for the first time.

Artis, was a life-long criminal. He had now turned to armed robberies as a way of "getting money." When he was arrested, the State was able to tie him directly to five armed robberies. If convicted, he faced life in prison. He was ready, willing, and able to make a deal.

"Just get me the best deal you can," he requested.

"The best deal they are offering you is 30 years with 15 in, before you're eligible for parole."

He thought about it for a moment, smiled and said,

"Tell them this. Tell them cut it to 15 with 5 all to run **concurrent** (together) and I'll give them a body."

"A body?" I queried. "Something you did or someone else?"

"Someone else, Mr. B. They've been looking for that shooting out of the east end. They charged some kid, but he was the driver, and they can't prove even that. I saw who smoked that kid and I can prove it for them."

"They are going to want specifics. Times, dates, how you know about it. And they are going to want a lie detector," I warned.

"No problem." He returned, with confidence. "I just want you to include one other thing. They have me here for five armed robberies. I did fifteen. I want to confess to all of them and have them wrapped up as part of the deal. No additional time and I want it in writing."

Artis' information checked out and his deal was made. It appeared that not only did Artis witness a gangland style shooting, he was also part of the planning. He was supposed to be the getaway driver, but declined in order to rob a gas station two blocks away. The robbery went so well that he thought he could get to the block and still make the loot as the getaway; maybe even create an alibi (if needed). He arrived on the block just in time to see the hit go down and to see the shooters.

"Some college kid who had just done a bid. They call him John Boy or something. Smoked this other kid, big time drug dealer. I heard him say it was his cousin. Did him right too. Three bullets to the head."

The State got its murderer. Artis got his deal and was back on the streets in 5 years. This time John, now known to the streets as "John Boy," took a plea. His lawyer was able to convince the State that if Artis was their eyewitness, they could lose John all together, so the State made him an offer he couldn't refuse. Seventeen years in prison with 7 years of parole ineligibility. I had to withdraw from both cases. Having previously represented John, and now representing Artis, created a conflict of interest.

Talking about misunderstood concepts in criminal law. The **plea bargain** is one such concept. The plea bargain is the criminal lawyer's best friend. When you, as a defendant, are innocent, you don't want to hear any mention about a plea. You listen to your lawyer regarding the plea because you have to. When your are truly guilty, all you want to hear is that someone is coming to you with a plea. You take it because you have to. Clients always want the benefit of the bargain; probation or time served. Often, that is an option that, if presented, you cannot and should not refuse. However, if the State is charging you with an offense and the plea offer will give you the same jail time or outcome that a trial will, there is no bargain. At that moment you take the matter to trial.

There was a young girl sentenced to 24 years in prison. Poor Kemba Smith. She allegedly took a plea that got her this sentence. It was on a drug offense, the maximum sentence of which is 25 years. No lawyer in his right mind should have put that plea through. Reports say that she was told that if she pleaded guilty, she would be facing up to 25 months. On appeal, every jurist hearing the appeal, should have seen this as incompetence or a sell-out by her attorney, overcharging by the government and foolishness by the Court that would accept such a plea. But this young girl (who had no prior involvement with the system) was sent to prison and suffered as her minor son grew into adolescence without his momma. Fortunately, someone saw past this cruel legal joke. The support she engendered around the country put pressure on the government to address this miscarriage of justice. They never did but, fortunately, she was pardoned by President Clinton after serving 6 years in prison.

When a plea is on the table, there are some basic questions that must be considered.

1. What are the proofs against you? I really do not care at this point if you committed the crime or not. Presumably, I am going to ask you if there is a number (sentence) out there that you feel you can live with. If you say no, then I am still going to negotiate the matter based on what I see in the Government's/State's proofs against you.

2. What are you facing if you lose at trial? If you are facing life in prison and the offer is 15 years, every lawyer in the phone book is thinking you are a fool if you do not take the deal. We could care less if you are innocent. Some of us will literally beg you to take it and twist every emotional arm you have in order to get it done.

3. Is there any discretion the prosecutor can exercise that I can use to your benefit? Most prosecutors have what is referred to as "prosecutorial discretion." This means that they have the authority, in the interest of justice, to negotiate pleas and can adjust the numbers based on their case. Attorneys in the real world spend a lot of time getting to know their government colleagues. We ask for favors, we beg for favors, we plead for pleas, all in an effort to get the deal that we believe is best for the client. Sometimes all it takes is a favor and another case quickly bites the dust. Unless of course you are in the federal system where the prosecutors (DAGs) are so afraid of offending the sentencing guidelines that the only real bargain is cooperation.

The biggest impediment to working out reasonable pleas is the legislature. In their fictitious, often fabricated wars on crime, they single-handedly have made almost every necessary tool of the system subject to their whims and political agenda. In the court, the judge gets to meet a defendant. This judge is supposedly trained and is supposedly able to make sound legal judgments. You also have a prosecutor who has reviewed the facts of his or her case, assessed its merits, and the total circumstances surrounding the crime. This prosecutor is also trained and has a mandate to seek justice. Finally, there is a defense attorney who wants the best light put on the face of his or her client so that where there is some discretion to be exercised, everyone who has the ability to judge, is making an informed, reasoned argument or decision. Unfortunately, all this training and hands on experience means nothing. The people who are in the trenches everyday are stifled by mandatory terms, legislative enactment's, three strikes laws, sentencing guidelines, and a host of other laws and regulations. These add nothing to the process, but they look good for some politician who has never met anyone charged with a criminal offense who he did not think was deserving of prison (except maybe his son, daughter, stock broker, accountant, or if you are in the DEA, maybe a wife or two).

I am so sick of judges and prosecutors saying, "Counsel you know that I have no discretion in this matter." I want to ask them, "So what are you here for? Hell, anyone can sign papers."

The integrity of the profession and of due process is being lost in political debates on crime and in legislative hallways. I shake my head in disgust every time I hear a politician or police chief say that crime is up or down. It's a political fabrication that is used to score emotional points with uninformed citizens. This fabrication is as much based on the manipulation of the economy as it is on the manipulation of the numbers. Crime is up when unemployment is high. Crime goes down when people have a sense of stability, a job. Crime is down means that the number of arrests are down, not the number of crimes committed. So if the government (executive) wants to scare the public into bolting their doors in fear, a couple of good "sweeps" in the right community will do the trick. Or maybe, they'll just declare another "war" on crime. (If you know who and how to ask, any police department will tell you this). While all this manipulation is going on, no one is informing the public that these politicians are using crime as a way to employ or revitalize rural economies through prison construction.

(These are the kind of games being played with your life and mind and you still cannot find the courage or intelligence to resist this criminal justice game).

Remember DC? DC was 18-years-old when he was busted for possession with the intention of distributing 100 vials of crack cocaine. He was the "runner" for the "big time drug dealer" we spoke about earlier. DC looked up to him and he would often tell DC that he was too young to get prison, if he got busted. DC, following his arrest, was sentenced to 3 years in prison. He was released after serving 9 months. He entered prison certain that his "boy," John's cousin, had set him up.

When he came home, he decided that he was going to get his life in order. He got two jobs and worked tirelessly until he was off parole. He moved in with his girl and they had a child. He was 24-years-old and, finally, beginning to do well. One night, while he was on his way home, he was stopped by an old friend who wanted to know if he wanted to go out and party. DC hadn't been out in a while, so he agreed. He went home, showered and changed, and when his old friend arrived, he was ready to party. He walked over to the car and noticed that there were three "brothers" in the vehicle he did not know. He sat in the front passenger seat and his old friend introduced him to the fellas; his "cousins" out of New York. They were going to the party too. However, they wanted to go to the South side of town to cop some weed, or so they said. DC used to "hustle" out there, so he agreed to show them.

"While we were there, this one guy named Artis pulled out a gun and they started robbing the drug dealers on the block. I didn't know what to do. They left me in the car and before I knew what was going on they had robbed everyone and were heading back to the car. One of the block boys refused to give up his money and Artis shot him. I panicked and tried to drive off, but I put the car in reverse and ran into a pole. They jumped into the car and told me to drive. At first, I hesitated. Then Artis put the gun to my head and said, 'DRIVE NIGGA.' So I drove off. We never did make it to a party. I asked my 'friend' why he did it and he just said everything would be cool. Artis said he could rob a drug dealer anytime because they can't report you to the police. The next day, I found out that the kid Artis shot had died and that some of the people from the block were saying that I was a part of it. I wasn't. I knew that kid all my life."

Poor DC. He had no clue how deep he really was in it. He was charged with felony murder, murder, and armed robbery. He tried, in every way that he knew, to convince everyone that he knew nothing about what happened. He cooperated with the authorities as best he could to show that he was not associated with the robbers. He was eventually indicted. His mother and father believed in him. His girl stood by him. But he was now back in the criminal justice system, and as I've told you, no one else really cared.

A **felony murder** conviction at trial is a mandatory 30 years in prison. The judge has no discretion to change it, even if he wanted to. Felony murder means that in the course of committing a felony (robbery) someone is killed. This killing can happen during the course of committing the robbery (as in DC's case) or in the immediate flight after the robbery or felony. For example, DC accidentally runs someone over following the robbery. If that someone dies, even though he wasn't an intended victim, DC could be convicted of felony murder. Armed robbery comes with a maximum of 20 years and a mandatory minimum of 5 years without parole. Again, the judge has no discretion to change it. The only thing that could change it is an outright acquittal at trial or a plea bargain.

The prosecutor investigated the matter and determined that it was "possible" that DC did not know what was going on. After all, none of the "New York" boys, when arrested, even knew his name. However, the prosecutor also determined that she had the necessary facts to prove DC was involved as the getaway driver and "point man" to the satisfaction of a jury, should DC elect to go to trial. These facts came from his "old friend" who had confessed to get a deal, and part of that deal was implicating poor DC as the getaway driver.

"But I didn't have a gun, I didn't know what was going on and he's lying on me."

"Son, do you understand the concept of **accomplice liability**?"

"No."

"An accomplice is someone who aides and/or abets. Someone who helps someone else commit a crime. For example, let's assume that the jury believes you showed them how to get to the area where the robbery was committed. Potentially that's enough to show that you helped in the robbery. That's what they mean when they call you a 'point man'. They will argue that all of your actions that night show that you shared the intention to rob with a weapon and that, they will try to show by circumstantial evidence. And yes, they will call your 'friend' to testify against you."

"But I didn't know they were going there to rob anybody."

"I understand that, but do you want a jury hearing that you were taking them there to buy weed? Jurors could believe that you didn't know, but if they don't, you're gone. And you have to remember only you can testify to that and once you take the witness stand, your prior record will be exposed to the jury. Also, who actually has the gun doesn't matter in the real world, son. As an accomplice, the law treats you as if you are the principal."

"What does that mean?"

"If I have a gun and they can prove you are down with me, you 'wear' the gun and the result of the use of a gun (the murder) as if you had the gun or used the gun yourself. That's what it is to be an accomplice and that's what they are charging you with. The shooter can take his plea bargain and get less time than you, if you lose at trial."

The plea offer was 20 years in prison with an 8 year period of parole ineligibility. We negotiated it down to 15 with 6. There was a strong likelihood that if DC had gone to trial, he would have been convicted and sentenced to the mandatory minimum of 30 years. His mother and father pleaded with him to take the deal. DC was innocent and determined not to. Finally, his girl, through her begging, crying, and pleading, convinced him to take the deal, so that he could be a part of the baby's life, someday.

In order to take a plea, you have to tell the judge what it is that you did that makes you guilty. This is called establishing a "factual basis" for the acceptance of the plea bargain. If you cannot establish a factual basis, that is admit to the crime and describe it, the plea is invalid. DC was not a part of the plan or the robbery, but he pleaded guilty to it, admitting that he was a part of the plan and the getaway driver.

"My mother didn't raise me to lie." he told me.

"I know son. And I understand how you're feeling right now."

"All day, all I do is cry and pray. I keep saying the same prayer over and over. 'Please Lord help me understand what is happening to me and help me deal with it like a man.' But I know I didn't do this crime."

"Son," I responded. "This isn't about whether or not you did it. I know it sounds strange, but it's not about you. It's about the system, and believe it or not, you just put yourself in the best position to have a life, a future."

At his sentencing DC was asked, by the judge, if he had anything to say. He wanted to say something. He had even written down what he wanted to say so that he wouldn't forget anything. But the words would not come out. He just could not stop crying long enough to say anything.

Watching a grown man or woman cry that you think may be innocent, but you know, in your heart, would be convicted if he or she went to trial, is a numbing, humbling experience. Watching an innocent person sentenced to life or one day in prison will make you cry, if you have a heart. I have seen and done a lot of crying. With the latter, you cry outwardly because you know there is no justice. With the former you cry inside because you cheated the system and it still won.

The Jury Is Still Out

The most misunderstood concepts in the criminal justice system are the **presumption of innocence** and **reasonable doubt**. I cannot tell you how many times I have been to lectures across the country or in colleges, churches, or high schools explaining this concept.

Many of the future leaders of America, when confronted with the concept of the presumption of innocence, will ask, "If a person is presumed innocent, why does he have to post bail or even be arrested?" It's a good question, but it is a mental exercise not really worth debating. The simple reason being, in the real world, you will never see this presumption of innocence.

When a person is arrested, it is supposed to be because he or she is suspected of committing a crime. A reasonable suspicion that a crime has been committed, and that you are the person who committed it, is called probable cause. At that moment, you have entered the criminal justice system and no one cares about your protestations of innocence. Bail is set (where appropriate) because the court is trying to ensure that you will appear and participate in the criminal justice process. Who cares if you're innocent? You are in it until the system lets you out.

You are then dragged into numerous court proceedings, arraignments, status conferences, pretrial conferences, etc., and offered plea bargains to resolve the matter. You are presumed guilty in each and every one of these proceedings. Fortunately, if you can prove you did not commit the offense, you can produce your evidence and maybe someone will listen to you, short of telling you to produce it at trial when your life is literally on the line. Most of the time you are spitting into the wind, no one is listening.

Once I was involved with a matter that I was certain would resolve itself by way of dismissal against my client. It was clear, from any cursory review of the State's case, that he was innocent. When I was pointing out all of the flaws in the State's proofs, it was like I was talking to myself. (It gets like that a lot when the prosecutor's chief witness is a cop). In situations like this, I regularly imply how I will defend a case including a discussion of potential witnesses who would blow the case out of the water. The prosecutor immediately asked for the names, addresses, and identifying information on the "potential witnesses." I dug my heals in to test this concept of a presumption of innocence.

"Your Honor. Why should I give him the names of these potential witnesses?"

"Don't you think that the State is entitled to this information counsel? I thought you were looking to resolve this matter short of trial."

"I've already told him what they would testify to, if called. If someone was interested in resolving this matter, that should be enough."

But they weren't interested in resolving the case. Most jurisdictions have a rule of **reciprocal discovery**, meaning the defense has to provide the names of fact witnesses it intends to call at trial.

"Judge, I am not sure that you are interpreting that rule properly. After all, the presumption of innocence means that the defendant or the defense has nothing to prove. There is no obligation on my client to offer anything at trial to prove his innocence. I should not have to turn anything over. I should not have to respond to anything until the State puts on some case. Therefore, the only reason the State would need this information now would be to rebut a defense that I don't, by law, have to put on or, as I suspect, to harass/intimidate these people."

The judge dug his heals in also.

"Counsel, you have ten days to provide the names of the witnesses to the State or I will bar you from calling them as witnesses at trial."

At almost every jury trial, the judge will give jurors what are called **preliminary instructions**. These instructions include an explanation of the concept of the presumption of innocence. The Court will normally say, "The defendant X stands accused by way of an indictment. The indictment is not evidence of his guilt, in fact, under our system a defendant is presumed or assumed to be innocent throughout the entire trial and the State has the burden of proving the charges beyond a reasonable doubt. The defendant has NO obligation to prove his innocence or even to offer any explanation or defense at all."

Cynical me. Every time I hear this instruction, I am thinking just like most jurors (who are honest enough to admit it) "Yeah right. If I have to assume he's innocent, why are we here?" The concept is dismissed almost immediately in favor of what common sense tells the juror to do. Jurors immediately begin to make value judgments that cut right to the heart of how they will perceive a case.

Most lawyers recognize this and prepare for it immediately. We dress our clients up depending on the type of jury we expect. The good lawyers recognize that image is everything and most jurors are not thinking "poor innocent fella." O.J. wore a different suit to court each day of his trial. It made him look successful, like he belonged on Wall Street, not in prison. The Menendez brothers sported sweaters. It made them look like school boy victims, not like money grubbing, homicidal maniacs.

White people expect to see a black defendant in a criminal matter. Black people are expecting to see one as well, but they enter the courtroom hoping that they know him personally, giving them an excuse not to serve. White people expect to see a white prosecutor and defense attorney. Blacks and Latinos want to see a black or Latino lawyer of any kind and really pull for him or her to do well, so when they vote to convict, they can say, "but he had a good lawyer."

If the defendant is a black male, white jurors expect him to have a criminal past. Black people expect him to be inarticulate. If the defendant is Latino, everyone is waiting for his, "I don't speak English, I don't understand defense." Latino jurors battle with being loyal to the brother or to the system more than other ethnic groups. They are often confused by the process and want to be seen as not showing favoritism based on race or ethnicity, so long as that lack of favoritism benefits the State.

Whites have no such problem. They give every benefit of any doubt to a white defendant and since they believe that most minorities are criminal minded, they give the benefit of the doubt to the State when it is a black or Latino male defendant. Blacks are perhaps the most confused and confusing jurors. I can't tell you how many times I have been in court while white lawyers are begging to have a black face on their jury. They are hoping that the "brother" or "sister" will be on the side of the black defendant they are representing. These lawyers never read Malcolm X or Carter G. Woodson, so they have no idea that many of the black jurors who qualify for service, hate the defendant who they see as embarrassing them in front of the good white people. When they are the only black face in the jury room, they too have loyalty struggles and many surrender rather than fight, even though the uniqueness of their experience in America demands that they hold fast to the presumption of innocence and reasonable doubt.

Whites, blacks, Latinos, and Asians will more likely be loyal to the system based primarily on their level of education. The better educated a juror is, the more likely they are loyal to the system, which can work either way at trial, if the attorney understands perception. These, of course, are generalities but they are based on seventeen years of in-court experiences, so "peep this before your reap this."

All I am really looking for, when I select a jury, are open-minded people and people who have courage. Courage is needed because I need *you* juror to stand up in the jury room, bring your experiences to the other jurors and not punk out, no matter how many people (who have never walked in your shoes) say you're wrong. Unfortunately, the standard question is, "Can you be fair?" Invariably, the answer is that most jurors can be fair to the system, even the closed-minded. Jurors often have never seen anything resembling the criminal offense charged so the system (status quo), (that they were all educated to believe works) wins. And those who have experiences similar to a defendant or who know the community where the alleged crime occurred, do not stand up or do not make it onto juries (because the government will ALWAYS challenge this type of juror, excusing them from service). Basically, the usual suspects bite the dust at trial simply because jurors perceive them as the usual suspects.

There are many, many more judgments, perceptions, and expectations involved in a courtroom drama and most clients have no clue about how they are being perceived. They hear a judge say that they have a presumption of innocence and they think it means something. Get real!! If you are black or some other group where your "image" is already associated with crime, you will, in most instances, have to literally destroy the government's case (prove your innocence) before you get the benefit of the doubt. And even then, most lawyers will tell you, you can never predict what a jury might do.

One day, I was sitting in the lawyer's lounge, having a nervous sip of tea. I was awaiting a verdict in a trial. There was a knock on the door. I was summoned into the courtroom.

"We have a verdict counselors. Let's bring out the jury."

"The jury is present and properly seated, your honor."

"Madam foreperson, have you agreed upon a verdict?"

"We have sir."

"As it relates to Count One of the indictment, Murder in the first degree, how do you find?"

No matter how many times I try a case, no matter how confident I am of the work done on a particular case, I dread the wait of jury deliberations and swallow my tongue whenever I hear those words.

When I decided to take this matter on, I knew from my initial review of the case, that it would be as tough a case as I would ever try. The defendant rejected all plea offers, because "I'm innocent," and the discovery in the case was voluminous. For nearly three months, I reviewed a different aspect of the case daily, just to make sure that I didn't miss something. I visited and revisited the crime scene. It was a neighborhood I knew well, I grew up there. Photographs, statements, autopsy reports, ballistics; I digested them all. When trial started, I was ready. Reasonable doubt was there, I just had to do the job the way I was trained to do it and justice would prevail. Each day, I arrived at court at 9:00 a.m. (OK...9:05) and left at 4:30 p.m. From court, I went straight to the library preparing for the next day and reviewing that day's testimony. "Did I miss something?" "Where is the prosecution going with this witness?" "The judge was wrong, that ruling did not apply, and here's the case that shows it."

I stayed in the library until maybe 10:00 p.m., only to return to the office for more review and preparation. Often, I fell asleep in the office and would be awakened by my wife who would call first thing in the morning to make sure I was still alive or had a change of clothing. I'd rush home just in time to kiss the kids before I had to run back to court and wage war. I have since repeated this set of circumstances numerous times because it is what is required when you take someone's life in your hands. I took on this case and with every case I am determined to do the job and do it right.

"As to Count One, Murder in the first degree, We find the defendant...NOT GUILTY."

I am trying not to celebrate too much, but I am very excited because I have the acquittal that I worked so hard to get. The client cannot control himself. He was facing 30 years to life in prison, just 10 seconds ago. Now, he is a free man. During the trial, I had established a tremendous amount of respect for the prosecutor handling this matter. She was bright, articulate, thorough. A class act. I was certain that she had put as much work and preparation into the matter as I had, and frankly, I was equally proud of the job she did in presenting this matter to the court. I looked to my right and could see the anguish on her face as the jury foreperson read off a series of "not guilty" verdicts to lesser-included offenses. As the client and I embraced, I looked directly into the eyes of the mother and sister of the victim. The tears were flowing steadily down their faces.

These are always the forgotten victims.

The jury was excused by the Court and my client was taken away by the court officers. He would be set free for the first time in two years. I slowly gathered my notes, books, and briefcase, hoping that the courtroom would clear out before I was ready to leave. The judge congratulated me on a job well done. He and I fought everyday during the trial. Sometimes our confrontations would become heated, but never personal (I hope). He had a job to do and no matter how often I disagreed with his calls in the courtroom, or his interpretation of the law, I always sensed that he had researched the law thoroughly and was prepared. The court officers nodded as I walked past, acknowledging that I had done a good job. As I approached the exit to the courtroom, the prosecutor and I made eye contact. It is customary and polite to shake the adversary's hand following a trial. We hugged. We both had fought the good fight. Our jobs were done. She and I both had to learn from this moment and move on to the next case. Frankly, I wasn't sure I wanted to. I learned that as criminal trial lawyers, we do not just try cases, we hold people's lives in our hands on all sides of the table.

In the hallway, I had to walk past the family of the victim. They truly believed that my client shot and killed their family member, their loved one. They spoke softly as I passed by. Proud, gracious people. The tears still flowed from their faces. I spoke back not really knowing what to say. I felt like maybe I should apologize, but I kept walking, looking for someplace to deal with all the emotions battling inside of me. I found a telephone and called the only person I ever think of at times like this.

"Hello."

"Hey baby."

"Hi daddy. When you coming home?"

My daughter's voice was disarming, I didn't expect her to answer the telephone. But her innocence quickly brought me back down to earth. She could care less about a trial. In fact, she wished I had a "real job" so I could be home more. After all, I missed her tenth birthday because of this trial.

"Let me talk to your mother."

"OK. Bring some ice cream when you come. Vanilla. Bye."

In the background I could hear,

"Mommy, it's daddy. He doesn't sound so good. He must have lost."

Mommy came to the phone.

"Hey there husband."

"Hey cutie. I'm on my way home. Want anything?"

"You heard that baby, vanilla ice cream."

Finally, I smiled. I needed to.

"How did your trial go?"

"We won."

"Really? You don't sound like it."

When I finished with the telephone conversation, I was feeling much better. My wife and daughter's voices allowed me to take off my lawyer hat and begin to relax. I went outside to the parking lot. In that lot were five of the jurors from the case. I tried to avoid them, but they were determined to speak with me.

"Mr. Bashir, Mr. Bashir. Can we talk to you?"

"Hi folks. Normally, I don't talk to jurors outside of court. Honestly, I'm not even sure if it's proper."

"Just answer a couple of questions please."

"Sure, if I can. Just don't ask me if I think he did it." I joked.

Everyone laughed and I listened, and learned.

"Did you dress the defendant in urban wear as part of your strategy?"

The client was 19-years-old with an eighth grade education. He had no family support during the year I knew him and had never worn a tie in his life. As usual, he had allegedly given a confession to murder, and since it was coming in as evidence at trial, I was sure that he would take the witness stand to explain his side. He could not speak a clear sentence in the King's good English and having him look like a choir boy and sounding like a hood rat (yo, naameen, like, you know and shit, I was like boom, Nigga was like yo) would easily be seen through by a jury. When he testified, the judge admonished him 15 times for cursing and it was my argument that since the statement didn't have one "motherfucker" or one "yo", this kid could not have given the confession that was before the jury.

"No, it wasn't a strategy per se. It seemed like the only way to get you to see this kid for what he really is. Inarticulate and ghetto hard."

"If you didn't put him on the witness stand, you know you would have lost."

"Really? Why is that? The same holes were in the State's case. The same witnesses were cross-examined and their inconsistencies shown."

"Yeah. But he just looked guilty. We all thought so from the beginning."

"So when the judge told you the defendant had the presumption of innocence, what did that mean to you?"

"Well, he also said use your common sense. Sometimes you can tell a lot from just looking at a person."

"Are you saying that all of you thought he was guilty before the State's case was even put on?"

"Honestly," one gentleman interrupted, "I had my mind made up after the prosecutor's opening."

"And all my brilliance and good looks didn't change your mind?"

"Maybe that's why you won."

Everyone laughed again. The more we talked, the more I wanted to know more about jury deliberations. So I let them continue.

"One of the jurors (a female) thought that you must be a private lawyer. She said you're too slick, too good, to be a public defender."

"What do you think?"

I asked, because in jury trials you never know what a juror will latch onto and what they perceive as important. Once a juror told me that my tie turned her off. Another juror said, he could feel that the lawyer (in the case he deliberated on) did not believe half of what he was arguing.

This, he said, he could tell by the lawyer's body language and sloppy dress.

"That kid can't afford a private attorney, he had no family come to court on his behalf, so his family must think he's guilty. I mean I wouldn't pay for a lawyer and then not show up, so you must be a public defender."

"Maybe I'm just a good samaritan who does this kind of thing pro bono on occasion because I believe in the process."

"Yeah! Sure!," an elderly juror responded. The others just laughed.

"Do you really think the police lied under oath?" They continued.

"That's a jury question. I have to trust you on that. I put the question back to you."

"Well, I understand your argument. And I do see some inconsistencies in their testimony. But do I really think that a cop would risk it all, fake a confession for this kid? I wouldn't."

I stood there thinking, "Risk what all?" No one prosecutes cops for lying on the witness stand. Foolish me for thinking that everyone knows this or that everyone even understands the process we all say is a "search for justice." For twenty minutes, we discussed deliberations and I learned that they were deeply concerned about balancing the defendant's credibility against the "facts" presented by the State. The presumption of innocence left the case after opening statements and would only resurface as a final consideration, an afterthought.

"Ms. A, the black lady, she said she felt you had integrity. We agreed. Plus, I have never heard a closing argument like that. You were really good and convincing. So we gave the kid the 'benefit of the doubt.'" Again, they laughed.

"Oh I see. So basically you're saying that you waited here for me to make sure that my in-court persona was real and that I didn't pull the wool over your eyes. You want to know if I really am 'slick'."

I was incensed by the thoughts they were expressing, and I was sure my anger was evident on my face. But they pressed on with questions as if I had the responsibility of vouching for my actions and the alleged actions of my client. They saw me as the proverbial "house negro," the slave they could trust to monitor bad "field negros" like my client. Finally, I had enough. I wanted to get away or at least to the bottom line question.

"So I guess what you're looking to find out is if I believe he did it after all."

"Yes!" They said in unison.

At this moment I was not sure I could control myself. These people had been trusted to do justice, seek out the truth and they did nothing. The defendant could have been sent to prison for the rest of his life and been completely innocent. The family of the victim could have been watching a cold-blooded murderer walk free. Ordinary citizens had been left with a job to do and never gave the job the attention that must exist in order for the system to work. Don't get me wrong. I am not saying that all juries drop the ball. I am saying however, that as a defendant or a victim, you are relying on a process that can and often does let you and itself down. When it does, there's nothing you can do.

Angrily, I responded, "Let me put it to you this way. I had a job to do. I did the best I could do with what I had to work with. The prosecutor had a job to do. She also did the best she could with what she had to deal with. We will both go home and be back tomorrow ready to do another job. Nobody is going to let her off the hook tonight while she tries to explain to the victim's family, and to herself, what went wrong. So I won't let you off the hook either. You want me to tell you that you didn't let a murderer walk so you can feel better. Next time, don't worry about whether I'm a public defender or whether I'm more slick than smart. Do the damn job."

I paused to catch my breath, only to notice the surprised looks on their faces. It was as if they could not believe that they had read me wrong. "So much for integrity," I thought. I continued speaking.

"Now, I'm going home and take my 10-year-old daughter some vanilla ice cream. I'm going to tell her that daddy did a good job. When she asks, and she will ask, I'm going to tell her that the jury understood that the defendant is presumed innocent throughout the entire trial and that the jury understood that he gets the benefit of the doubt, if ANY reasonable doubt exist. In other words, they did their job too and the system worked the way it is suppose to. Now, I need one favor from you all. If I ever run into any of you on the street, treat me like the fool that I'm sure you think I am. Devalue my intelligence or disrespect me up front, so I don't have to waste my time with people who could give less than a damn about the truth. And until then...get the hell out of my face."

I know that these poor people didn't deserve my anger, but honestly, far too often I go to court hoping that the system will work the way I was taught that it is supposed to. Each day something about it rips the cover off this "justice for all" myth. The fate of countless men and women is being determined by judges, lawyers, prosecutors, police, juries, and a system whose fallibility is demonstrated in ways that I could never have imagined. Look at how self-righteous I had become. On any other day, I could care less about jury deliberations, especially if they came back with a not guilty verdict. Here I am now judging people who could have convicted the defendant or acquitted him and no one would ever know why. We would all just say the system worked. I had to remind myself that this system isn't about truth or justice, it's about winning, scoring points, and perception. Finally, I have surmised that only a fool wants this type of scrutiny, this type of judgment. A fool or a criminal.

Only three days had passed since the trial, when the client came to my office. He had his girlfriend on his arm. I remember thinking how funny it was to see them together considering the fact that I had never heard one word from her during the year I was preparing for the trial. In fact, I heard she was sleeping with his best friend since she was sure he wouldn't be coming home for the next 30 years. Finally, we had a minute to talk.

"Mr. Bash, I just wanna say, like yo, like thanks for your help and shit. Been givin' you mad props in the hood. Gimme some cards. I told my peeps your shit is like off the hook."

"No need, little brother. Just do me a favor. Stay out of trouble."

"Word. I'm 'bout ta bounce in a few. Movin' to Atlanta next month, naameen."

"Good idea."

"Yo. You still my lawyer and shit right?"

"Why?"

"Like if I tell you something, like yo, you can't tell nobody right?"

"Depends. What's it about?"

"About the trial."

A strange sense of disgust and anxiety began to swell up inside of me. Throughout the last year, I had represented (to the best of my ability) a young man whose innocence of which I was certain. Frankly, I would have represented him with the same vigor and effort, if I believed he had committed the crime charged. My small part in the system demands that someone put the State's proofs/evidence to the test. You just cannot send people to prison because they look different or because they were in the wrong area or because they have an eighth grade education and can be manipulated by college-trained detectives. The system demands more. Proof beyond a reasonable doubt.

My job is just to show the reason to doubt. Once I do that, the jury MUST acquit. That's how it works, if it is ever going to work. It must work that way if you did not commit the crime and it must work that way even if you did commit the crime. The burden of proving all the elements of a crime is on the prosecution. There is no balancing. "I believe the cop more than I believe the defendant." A defendant can take the witness stand and lie through his teeth and still the State may not have proved its case beyond a reasonable doubt. Far too often, juries engage in a comparison of what weight to give to testimony and it flies in the face of the presumption of innocence and reasonable doubt.

Again, I paused for a moment. In that moment, I could see and feel the countless hours I had put into preparing for this trial. I recalled in my mind the time away from my family and the countless trips to the county jail visiting this client. I still feel the effects of the tension that surrounded the courtroom for two weeks of testimony and the sleepless nights of constant review and preparation. I closed my eyes to hold back my developing rage. I could see the anguish that the prosecutor and I both shared when we heard there was a verdict. I remembered the look on the faces of the victim's family (victims themselves) as they sat dumbstruck in the courtroom.

After all we had been through, what would he have to tell me now that he could not have told me over the past year? In any event, I really didn't want to hear it.

"That's done little brother. Let the past stay in the past."

"I just feel like, yo, like I gotta get this shit off. Yo like, I keep havin' bad dreams and shit. My mom is like, yo, 'you gotta make peace' and shit. I'm 'fuckin trippin,' naameen?"

"Brother, listen to me closely. Don't take this the wrong way. We are through with your case. I am through with your case. Do you know how hard I worked on your trial? How much time I put into it? My people saw me maybe twice during the whole trial and one of those times was for a minute on my daughter's birthday. You know she and I have the same birthday? But when a jury makes its decision, I have to get on with my life, win, lose, or draw.

Now, why am I telling you all this? You had every opportunity to talk to me about your case before and during the trial. I told you once that I will not do your jail time for you if we lose, so allow me to tell you one extra thing. I'm not carrying your emotional baggage now. If you're looking for absolution or forgiveness or anything like that, you got the wrong office, the wrong guy. Honestly, I don't give a shit about your bad dreams or you 'fuckin trippin,' and I ain't the Pope or a priest. That's not how I roll. So do me one last favor. Get the hell out of my face and my office! Believe it or not, this lawyer thing is what I do. It's not what I am. Come back in another life when you realize what you are. Your file and my door are now both closed."

Criminal Minded

When I first entered this profession, I was naïve in thinking that there is something called a "victimless" crime. Even though I often argue that the facts of a particular crime demonstrate no victim, I'm not so foolish anymore.

Each and every moment, I understand the criminal justice system more and more through the eyes of victims. I walk streets littered with victims of drug distribution (men, women, and families that I grew up with who my kids tell me, look old enough to be my father or mother). Children who cannot sit still in school because mom "experimented" with drugs while she was pregnant and the baby is now living a life of uncertainty. Young boys who want so much to be like their dad that they expect nothing more from life than to "sling rocks," wear "Jordans" or "Tims," or "bust a cap" in someone. I get on elevators with victims of the perception of crime. Women who maneuver their handbags away from my side or get off on the wrong floor rather than be confronted by their perception of crime. (And I'm the one in the suit).

These people are victims of a perception created by racism, the media, and/or some punk who has the same complexion as me, but has self-hate in his heart. I play ball in communities that (in my lifetime) had trees, but are now a collage of empty lots, torn down crack houses, and bricks. The children of that community are victims of criminal and police intimidation, governmental neglect and low/no self-expectations. Victims.

When someone is killed, not only is that life destroyed, all of the lives he or she touched are changed forever.

There is the son who no longer has a role model and who now has to start life all over because everything his father promised to build for his future has been destroyed.

There is the daughter who used to take walks with her daddy who now, has no concept of manhood to draw from as she grows into womanhood. She longs for the attention that he would always give. Just someone to make her feel special again. The seeds of self-doubt and dependency are now planted in her heart and mind as she searches for just the right hand to hold. Far too many hands will walk her to a bedroom, but few will ever walk her to the park, like daddy.

There is the mother who relied on her deceased son or daughter to take her to the grocery store. She's too tired, or distraught, or old to now begin doing these things for herself, and the child's untimely death only shows her how truly helpless she has become.

And the father who will forever feel like less than a man because he could not protect his son or daughter. After all, he was raised to believe that a "man" is the provider and protector of the family. These are all victims that you don't see and don't think about as a criminal. And there are many, many more.

When you steal from someone, you take away their sense of trust in everyone. You don't just steal their valuables, you take a part of their soul. It's sad to watch these victims as they check every door twice or bolt their windows before leaving home. It's insane for a mother to beg her son not to wear his "Iversons" to a party or display the chain she bought him for his birthday because she's afraid he may meet some thug with larceny in his heart and just might not make it home that night. They become victims and so does everyone that trusted them and everyone that they trusted.

That little girl or young woman you raped, penetrated, touched, can't move without thinking about the pain you caused her. She hates in the deepest and most confusing ways. Every man's touch is your dreaded touch. Every look from a man has a sexual/destructive motive. She eats excessively so that no man will find her sexually attractive again. Sometimes she never recovers and, if she's too young to properly interpret the pain, she grows up believing that destructive sex is all that a girl or a woman has to offer. So she bears the pain secretly while she works her way through relationship after relationship, four or five children from four or five men. Every friend is now a distant friend and everyone who comes into contact with her can feel her pain, sense her confusion, or her hate.

I once was in my office and a young boy (maybe 18) came in. He wanted representation. In his bag he had $15,000.00 in cash, and a kilo of cocaine. He wanted to pay me to hold the coke because the detectives were right behind him. Think about the arrogance this guy had! But he has the normal criminal mindset. "What you have makes you important." "I can buy or talk my way out of anything." He never saw me as a potential victim of his recklessness. I was only a way of keeping him out of trouble. At that moment, we had a conversation about crime that lasted for an hour. The cocaine stayed in the briefcase and I charged him $250.00 for my time, before I dismissed him from my office.

"Tell me this money, how often do you do this kind of thing? I mean sell cocaine."

"I'm in the game."

"So full time?"

"Yeah."

"Who do you live with?"

"Me, my mom, and my little sister."

"You supporting all of them with your dealing?"

"Pretty much. My mom is disabled. I know what you're thinking, my mom is down with this, but she ain't. I got into this to make some easy loot 'cause she can't work and that welfare shit is wacked. Do you know they make her walk down to this place and argue with her about how much she gets from SSI? If you think I'm a criminal those bitches are the criminals."

"No brother, I'm thinking what would your mom do if and when you get picked off. Everything you think you're helping her with is temporary and gone once you get busted."

"I'm handling that. Putting my money away just in case."

"You kidding right? Lawyers see cats like you coming a mile away. By the time you finish paying to get yourself out of trouble, all you'll have is more trouble. And think about it, where can you put money that the government can't find it? You still livin' in the projects right? With a brand new Escalade parked in the lot, right?"

"You hard Mr. Bash."

"I got one better for you. What happens when they charge your mom; disabled and in prison? What do you do with your little sister then? How do you spell 'HOE'? Brother, if and when they want you, they are coming for you and you are gonna leave a list of victims of your acts that will never recover from it because they can't be as street hard as you think you are. Boy, go home and look long and hard at your mom and little sister. If you care about them, find a real job and bust your ass. You don't have to hide that from cops and, who knows, you just might get them out of the bricks and into a better situation with a little hard work and patience."

But he really didn't look at his mom or sister. He looked at the lifestyle. It was about him and with criminals, it is always about YOU! You don't really care about your mom. If she's a victim, it's the price of the game. You don't really care about your baby's mother or the baby. While you are in prison complaining and calling collect, you don't get to see them crying every night not knowing how they are going to make it. You don't see all the "playas" hawking your girl like she's a piece of meat. You don't see your son or daughter (as they grow up on welfare) hating the fact that they have to go to the store with those coupons. Your baby, your "blood," has no direction. The whole town knows his daddy is a drug dealer, a murderer, an armed robber, or a rapist. Although your peers may think that's something "cool," everyone he comes into contact with (who hears his name) whispers behind his back. He hates his name, your name. Your girl is watching him grow up without a daddy, a male role model. She can't control him once he reaches 6-years-old. He's already "off the hook." She is looking older and older every time you see her because he is wearing her out. You have no bass in prison and when you're on the streets, he still has to deal with the hate that you produced. All the money, all the "juice" you think that you have, all the fine clothes you're supplying cannot help him when they ask him in school, "Children, tell me what your parents do for a living." He hates school already.

Now, your son is 10 and your daughter is 12. She has no one to protect her and some 23-year-old playa is on her. At 13, she's sexually active. You can see it in her walk when she visits you in the clack, your third time down. This "sucka" is promising her the world, the same promises you made to your girl. You know where he's headed and where she's headed. At age 13, she gets pregnant. You're 30 now and a granddad. Your daughter has no skills for a baby and this "joker" she's "doin" is on to the next young "piece of ass." Welfare again. The State is, once again, the man of the house. Motherhood is too hard for her. She's 14 with no motherhood skills and your girl has had about enough of her too. She's a child with a child, and she's feeling herself. She begins to experiment with drugs. She tries marijuana for a while and then crack cocaine. She can "cop" from your son, after all, he's now 12 and in the game...a chip off the old block. She likes crack. It's better than sex. She wants more and more. You can see the changes in her face. The color is leaving her. Her weight is slipping. "Man she used to be so pretty." That look that you saw on the faces of so many people you used to serve, is coming home, and it's your baby girl. You tell your son to stop serving her, to look out for her, but he's 15 now, and his own man. He loves the lifestyle like you did. He doesn't see her as his sister or as a victim, just as a customer. After all, she hooks him up with her friends; he gets some booty, she gets her cracks. Mom can't help either of them. She was relying on you when she had these babies and you "fucked up!"

At 17, your son is "picked off" by the police. His role model (you) is not around to tell him to keep his mouth shut or to educate him about the way the game is really played. The police suggest to him that if he tells them who he was selling for, they will let him go. Maybe he tells or maybe he doesn't. It really doesn't matter. Three weeks later his name appears in the **discovery** (report) of a major player. You read about this kingpin's arrest and begin to hear all the rumors. "Your boy gave him up." "Your boy can't be trusted." You know the game, so you know what's coming. You can't help. In prison, you may have finally found Allah or Jesus and you're trying to turn your life around. But all you can really do is pray for his soul because his ass is just about done.

One day, your girl tells you that your son has disappeared. He told her that he and his boys were going out. These are the same "boys" who he was selling for and with. The same "boys" he grew up with. One week later, he is found in a cemetery with a bullet to the back of his head. His hands were cut off. The autopsy shows that he was beaten nearly to death. Maybe, the bullet was a blessing. Your girl hates you now. You aren't there for her and you were never there for the kids. "You call yourself a man? You ain't shit!" All the money in the world cannot replace the self-esteem your kids never had because their father is a criminal.

Your girl finally decides to take up with a new guy. She wants/needs to feel important. After all, no brother with anything going for himself wants any part of her once they hear that she used to be your girl. This new guy has warrants from everywhere and he's not telling. He makes her feel like a woman, but her life is in danger each and every moment, and she doesn't have a clue. What matters to her is that he helps out with the bills, and he's there. He's a "stick-up kid" who uses crack or heroin to get a boost before he robs. Your baby girl still has her habit, even though little brother is gone. Her kids are living with your girl (grandma) and this new joker, who introduces baby girl to heroin in exchange for a sexual favor or two; so long as she doesn't tell mom.

This is the family you produced. Somewhere out there, your acts or inactions touched many people. You never thought your "game" through, but it's not a game. People suffer from these games. Your girl cries everyday. She is alone and lonely; 36 going on 56. She says that she loves you, but she really hates everything about you.

When you start on this road of crime, there is no potential success, no potential future, and no matter what you put away, there are so many rainy days that you can never cover them all. At the end of this road, there is only one group that remains, victims. The person you robbed; the person you loved; the person you served; the person you trusted; the persons who trusted you; the person you killed; the persons you're killing. If you ever stop to look, you'll see that all you have created in this life is tragedy and victims. The question at the end of the day, is whether you have enough humanity in you to care. The true nature of a Man. Unfortunately, where you have been living for the past ten years, there are no men. You don't want to admit it and you strive hard in the "deen" or "for the lord." But in prison, you will always be nothing more than a slave or someone's bitch (even if that someone is the system itself).

Finally, your girl finds a job. Burger King is hiring. She has to work because she has always had to work. Work was never enough to support her and the kids, so she remained in the welfare system while she worked and while you bounced in and out of jail. The new man of the house likes this set up, but he has to get to work too. He doesn't care about her little $200.00 paycheck. At Burger King, he could rob the joint and pocket two "G's" easily. Who would know? He doesn't care that she likes this job.

So what if she's been doing it now for a year and she finally feels like she has some sense of self-worth? He's a criminal with the same criminal mindset you have. "I can get away with this." "I'm just trying to get paid." "We do what we gotta do to survive." Criminal minded; It's all about you. It has always been about you.

He hits the Burger King one night just after she leaves. He gets busted. In his wallet, he has her picture and telephone number. The police cannot prove she had knowledge of the robbery, but he is willing to say that she did, if he can get the right deal. She gets fired and winds up back on welfare. She's one public pretender away from prison as an accessory to robbery and welfare fraud. She now has two babies to feed. Your daughter's children. The youngest, 4-years-old, stays sick. She's a crack baby, they think and, just like your daughter, she has AIDS.

One morning, the telephone rings at your lawyer's office. He stops by the prison to visit you. Your last appeal has been denied. Parole was also denied. You sit in your cell thinking how the lawyer, the judge, the parole board, the system let you down. Words like "railroaded," "sold-out," "used," "VICTIM," race through your mind. You want these words to apply to you, but you know, in what's left of your heart, that it's bullshit.

In your cell you know there is no one left to "front" for. There, you hear your girl's voice over and over telling you, "You ain't shit!" And finally, it sets in. You're not a man. You're less than a man; less than a slave; less than shit. You're a CRIMINAL.

Ride or Die

As I sat down to complete this book I had to decide if I was trying to educate, to explain, or just to vent. I discovered that I needed to do all of the above. Allow me this opportunity to vent. And please, follow closely. I have a reputation of going around the block to get across the street. I like that reputation because each trip around the block teaches me something.

Constantly, I hear people spouting about the "Hip-Hop" culture and its impact on society. If I were in the music/entertainment industry, maybe making a billion bucks to bust some lame rhyme about some "hoes" or "bitches" or about getting into some too young girl's pants, I'd probably be singing the praises of "Hip-Hop." But I'm in the justice system and from where I sit…"Hip-Hop" is a fraud.

"These young brothas and sistas are just keeping it real." "This is the culture they know and they are just expressing it." "It's raw and uncut, from the streets."

Yeah right!!

Take a long look around you. Look at where the culture has come from and where it is headed. One day in court, I was unwittingly drawn into the conversation of two middle-aged men. Both wondered out loud, where "our values have gone." I had just completed the sentencing of a young boy who was involved in a gang related incident. He, and his red scarf, was sentenced to three years in prison. He gave up (ratted on) his crew so he got the best deal. (Another example of gang brotherhood). As I listened to the two gentlemen I couldn't help but wonder, out loud. "Brothers it's not about where our values have gone. It's a matter of where 'our values' came from."

Every child born in America has in some way been impacted by the images created around and about America's criminal culture. When I was a kid, I was a big "Gas House Gang/Bowery Boys" fan. I remember one movie that has stuck with me all of my life. It was called "Angels With Dirty Faces." The "Gang" costarred with James Cagney, aka Rocky Sullivan. Rocky was a child when he first got popped by the police for stealing (dirty coppers). He just couldn't get over that fence fast enough, like his friend, who later grows up to become a priest. Rocky does time and eventually, as a man, becomes public enemy number one. He is a hero to the "Gang," a group of street kids with limited prospects for future success. Imagine that. Even back in the '50s a gangster could be a hero to kids who felt like nothing really mattered, no one really cared. Rocky kills half the people in the movie and is eventually sentenced to die in the electric chair. Father "whatshisname" is fighting to keep the gang on the straight path, but they love his old friend, the criminal. He's larger than life. He's not just famous, he's infamous. They love the lifestyle he lives. They love his charisma; the way he walks and talks. He's large. He comes from among them, lives and works in their hood, and he's made it big.

Eventually, the debate comes down to—will Rocky go to the chair a tough guy and thus ensure the "Gang" will worship/follow him on his path? Or will he die a coward at the request of his old friend and thereby save these kids from idol worship, giving the good father a shot at redeeming these little "wannabe" gangster kids?

Rocky is no punk, but he knows he's gonna die, so on his way to the chair, he cries and begs for mercy. "Please, I don't wanna die." He dies like a coward. The "Gang" can't believe it. They are devastated. They turn to the father who confirms the reports. Rocky went out like a punk. The kids are jolted back to reality, saved from a life of crime. By changing his image, he saved a generation. Rocky died a hero. The End.

I won't try to explain the psychology of idol worship, but I will say this. It is no accident that the media profits off mob movies, serial killer movies, crime stories, etc. Equally, it is no accident that there is a proliferation of street gangs, serial killers, or violent crime. And do not be fooled by this reverse English that says the media is only showing or reporting what's going on out in the streets (with a little creative license). The media and societal violence are joined at the hip and the result is the devaluation of life in the real world. Americans view acts of violence so often that it becomes almost commonplace and thus, death/violence is not an issue, it's a forgone conclusion. The same arguments that are now being used to discuss, protect, justify the images (both positive and negative) fed to this generation, have been used to justify the images of every generation. Yet, when the smoke clears take a look at the society, the culture, the children, and only the foolish will argue that image means nothing.

I was truly convinced that I would be dead before I reached the age of 21. I had been told this so often that it had imbedded itself in my subconscious. I was first told this by a teacher in the fifth grade who thought that I should be placed in the special education program. He even showed me some magazine that verified that I wouldn't see my 21st birthday. I was well on my way to self-doubt, self-hatred, and special education until Lester Randolph, my fifth grade teacher, risked his career to save me, because he said I had potential. When I say he risked his career, I mean he literally got into a fist fight with the special-ed teacher in the hallway over me. I was blown.

Thereafter, I was assigned to Mr. Randolph's class because the school believed that he was the only teacher who could control me. I entered the fifth grade under the stipulation that if I didn't perform, my next stop was special-ed. He knew I was a thug, but each day he worked me, called on me, debated with me, and made me participate. He gave me the nickname, "Perry Mason" because I always had an argument. My self-image went from trouble maker to that of the teacher's pet. From the "smart ass" to the smart kid.

However, when I left school, I always had to return to the bricks. Poor black kids with no hope. Poor Latin kids with no hope. Poor white kids with no hope, but with at least the security that they weren't blacks (although they "acted like brothas"). I grew up in a generation that was educated to believe:

"If you're white you're alright, if you're yellow it's mellow. If you're brown stick around, but if you're black, get back."

So all many of us really had was our image. In the projects, I was a tough guy. All any of us there ever really wanted to be was "duke" of the court. Everyday, I had to fight to maintain my image, to maintain my respect. Gang fights were common and you participated even if you weren't in a gang. The simple reality that we all knew was that you could not live there and be seen as an outsider or "not down." Knives were the weapon of choice. I always carried a stick or a belt with one of those heavy iron buckles on it, and I knew just how to use it.

By the time I was 17, I knew death firsthand. Wayne, the guy who taught me how to carry a football, was stabbed to death. Bates, the guy who taught me how to protect the basketball with a reverse dribble, got his throat slashed. Steve, just good people, died mysteriously in New York. Some say it was a drug deal gone bad. Barbara, a real cutie, took a bullet from an ex-boyfriend that ended her life at 16, but did not end the crush I had on her. This list began to grow and grow and I began to believe that before long, it would be my turn. Fortunately, I had parents, teachers, and mentors who fought as hard for me to believe in something as I had fought to stay alive. They didn't give up, so neither did I. The more educated I became the more I didn't need to participate in the culture that surrounded me. I was still a thug inside, but I began to like the idea of being an educated thug.

One day, all the "fellas" gathered in the courtyard of the Pioneer Homes housing project, as we normally did, to play ball. While we were "hoopin," the police raided the project, guns drawn. They ordered everyone to get up against the wall, at gunpoint. We did as we were told. All of us except my friend Larry. Larry wasn't having any of that "bullshit." This was his court and we had done nothing to deserve the pat downs, searches, or the threats we were now under.

"Fuck it," he said. "If you gonna shoot me then do it, or get the fuck out of my face." I looked over at my brother, who is now a prominent and highly respected attorney himself, and we both had the same look on our faces. "Damn Larry is gonna get us all killed." In somewhat of a surreal moment, we both laughed as much out of fear and temporary insanity as anything else. We were kids, maybe 17-years-old, and we really didn't grasp the seriousness of life and death. But I learned something valuable in that moment. Life, everyone's life, is something to be respected, cherished. When you are shown no respect or, put another way, if everyone disrespects you, then what do you really have that's worth living for? When you determine that respect is important, you then decide that it's worth maintaining and you won't give it up without a fight. Larry had reached the point to where he was tired of being disrespected, so "fuck it."

As an attorney, I've learned to reflect on every trip around the block because these trips make me what I am. One day, I was late for court. So that you know, that is not unusual for me. I had a number of matters in one county and could not make it to my next county before noon. As a courtesy to the court, I called the judge's chambers. They responded:

"You can't come in today, Mr. Bashir."

"Sure I can, I'll just be there this afternoon, if you don't mind."

"No, you don't understand, we have an incident here. No one is allowed in or out."

The incident was like none I'd ever heard of before. Two young men were on trial for drug distribution. One of the police officers involved in the case was scheduled to testify that morning against the defendants. When the officer arrived in the court, he did what most witnesses do, he waited outside of the courtroom for his name to be called. As he waited, he was approached by another young man. Reports indicate that this young man pulled out a handgun, pointed it to the head of the officer, and squeezed off a round that instantly caused the officer's death. The shooter was able to escape out of the courthouse after a shootout that wounded two other officers.

However, he didn't get far and was eventually captured.

As I read through the reports in this case, I began to get the sense that at some point this young man had determined that it was time to die. He had given away many of his possessions and began to talk in terms that suggested that life now had nothing to offer him. I read the discovery over and over and the one thing that came to my mind each time was Larry saying, "fuck it."

This young man was indicted and tried in a death penalty case. As I got deeper into the investigation of this case, I began to evaluate the issue of life and death from a very familiar perspective. The criminal who shot the cop, it turned out, was a reputed drug dealer. The officer, it was rumored, worked for this drug dealer. On the streets, the word was that the cop was killed because he turned on his "people." For the shooter it was a simple issue of respect. None of the evidence suggesting criminality associated with the cop was admitted at the trial. The jury found this cop killer guilty of the murder, but did not vote for the death penalty. He was sentenced to life in prison without the possibility of parole. Another death sentence.

At the sentencing phase of the trial, it was suggested that the shooter was insane, mentally disturbed at the time. I didn't sense that at all. I felt him. I grew up with him. I am a part of a generation, a culture that, in many ways has given up on the system for one reason or another. I have lost friends to heroin and crack epidemics, Vietnam, police brutality, the street and corporate America. Many of my generation are just lost in the reality of making ends meet leaving no time or reason to change the world or even understand the world they are leaving for their children. I didn't agree with this shooter's sick solution, but I understood it. In a court of law, he may have been crazy, but on the street he was just another kid with nothing to live for and the only thing he had worth respecting was his image, whatever that was, and like Larry he would die or kill to protect it. I represent a lot of kids who think their "rep" or image, their "turf" or "colors" matters.

(I represented the co-defendant in this matter who was charged with the murder as an accomplice. My client was supposed to be the getaway driver for a guy who drove his own car to the courthouse that day, never expected to get out of the courthouse alive that day, never saw my client that day, and was willing to die to make a point. The proposition of a getaway driver in another car was absurd but, as with many of these type of cases, the State found some other drug dealers who were willing to testify that my client told them he was down with the shooting. They got damn good deals for that group of lies. Because he faced life in prison without the possibility of parole and because he was indicted in two other matters for first degree drug crimes—facing life there too, and because he was scared as hell, the client went with the plea "offer he couldn't refuse." He immediately regretted it, but maybe he saved his own life.)

Whenever I lecture, I get asked about the death penalty and I recall this case. Politicians tell you that they "really believe that the death penalty deters crime." They are lying. What they really believe is that support for the death penalty is an issue dear to the hearts of those in this country who vote. So being the "hoes" that they are, they support it. No one, criminal minded or otherwise, is out there thinking, "If they didn't have a death penalty in this state, I'd kill you." Or "Damn, I'd better not kill these Wendy's employees who saw my face because I might get the death penalty." It is a ridiculous proposition.

What is a **death penalty** anyway? The legislature has decided in many states, that some crimes should be punished with the ultimate punishment, your life. However, almost universally, the decision to charge a case as death eligible is left to the discretion of the prosecutor. Simply stated, the case is reviewed by the prosecutor and he/she gets to decide whether it should be tried as a death penalty case. One of the factors, called "special circumstances," to be considered in determining if the case is death eligible is the nature of the crime. The more heinous the crime, the more likely the charged person will face death. A sniper randomly picks victims from an undisclosed location, and kills them with no reason or rationale. A young boy is tied to an alter and beaten to death because he is gay. The more vicious or socially repugnant the case, the more likely the defendant will face death as punishment.

Other considerations for the death penalty are such things as murder for hire, premeditation, the death of more than one person committed during the same action, the vulnerability of the victim, and the murder of a cop in the performance of his/her duty. In almost all death penalty cases, the defendant must face trial on the merits of the case and, if convicted, will then go through a death penalty trial or phase. The death penalty does not exist in all states and the federal system is, under the tremendous pressure of the Executive branch, redefining what makes up a death penalty case on a daily basis. Terrorism resulting in death is dominating the debate, followed closely by violence related to narco trafficking.

In a death penalty case, the process of determining whether to sentence to death is basically the same as the sentencing in any other case. Before sentencing anyone, the Court or in a death penalty case, the jury, must determine the **aggravating and mitigating circumstances**. This means that they must decide what about you, your background or the nature of the case hurts you and what about your background, helps you. Some of the aggravating circumstances to be considered are:

1. The nature of the offense. (Was it extremely cruel or unusual?)

2. The need to deter you and others from this type of activity. (Clearly a waste of breath in most criminal matters. This factor implies that the Court or the Legislature is sending a message to you and others who commit similar crimes. It's the same kind of "tough on crime" crap you hear every time someone is seeking an elective office. If the person is criminal minded, you haven't deterred anything no matter what the sentence).

3. Whether the defendant has prior involvement with the criminal justice system. (I read some statistics that said that nearly one in every three black males will have been involved in the criminal justice system before they reach the age of 30. Also, if you are poor, you have a 50% more chance of getting involved in the criminal justice system. And that more than 65% of all those incarcerated in prisons have less than a 10th grade education and no job at the time of their incarceration. You get the drift yet?).

4. The likelihood that the defendant will commit another offense. (If you are criminal minded, it is very likely. If you do not see a future for yourself outside of the bricks of Newark, or the gangs of LA, or your heroes are the Rocky Sullivan/Nino Browns of the world, it is very likely you'll commit other offenses).

Some mitigating factors are:

1. The defendant's lack of prior involvement in the criminal justice system. (It makes sense, but you can throw this one out once you get that first conviction, and it will matter if you were convicted as a juvenile regardless of what your lawyer and your friends tell you).

2. Whether the defendant was cooperative with the authorities, i.e., the police. (I always smile when I hear this one because it usually means that he "ate cheese" to help himself. He ratted on someone, became an informant or cooperating witness and now is getting the benefit of being a criminal who won the race to the prosecutor's office. Federal drug crimes are almost universally tried with these people as witnesses. At the end of the case, they are expecting a 5K1 letter which authorized the judge to move away from the sentencing guideline. In Connecticut, I witnessed this firsthand. People facing life in prison, were getting probation to testify that there was a drug conspiracy and racketeering enterprise run by my client. It didn't matter that these witnesses told a different story about the organization each of the three or four times they testified. They knew as long as they cooperated, they had a good chance of going home because cooperation doesn't necessarily mean telling the truth).

3. Whether incarceration or the penalty to be imposed will result in a substantial hardship to the defendant or others. (Give me a break. No one really cares about this if you are young, poor, minority, and/or undereducated. However, if you are white, well-educated, employed, with privilege or family backing, this factor becomes a major argument at your sentencing. Amy Grossberg and her boyfriend come to mind immediately. Can you believe these two jerks were ordered to counsel other kids as part of their parole? Can't you just hear them saying, "I put the baby in the garbage and left it to die so please come to me when you need to make decisions. I understand.")

There are numerous other factors that are argued and considered during a sentencing. However, in a death penalty case, the factors are properly left to the jury to decide, while in your run of the mill crime, a judge decides. A few years back, I went to the trial of twin drug dealers in Maryland to witness this phase. One brother, the more dominant personality by all accounts, begged for the life of his brother. He told the jury that all the murders that were committed and all the lives they destroyed were at his order, not his brother's. Even I was moved by this plea. The jury voted. The "Twin Terrors" are doing life in prison.

The problem with the death penalty is that determining whether a person should live or die is part of a system that is seriously flawed. The government, when choosing to prosecute, considers race and status in their decision. They will say they don't, but race and status permeates the system. No one will admit that either. Until they do, no serious debate on the death penalty will be forthcoming. So debate this—If you are black and/or poor, you are more likely to face the death penalty and that decision originates with the prosecutor's office. Further, many of these prosecutions are politically motivated. The more public outcry, the more likely a death penalty case. (Young sniper suspect Lee Malvo was taken to Virginia where there is a death penalty and it would not have mattered one bit if 20 people were killed in a non-death eligible state prior to the one death in Virginia).

Additionally, when most of the death penalty trials are reviewed and reversed, the record often reflects that the defense lawyer did a terrible job. Many of the people trying criminal cases are not qualified to try cases of this magnitude, nor do they have the courage it takes. No investigation, no experts, no DNA testing, and no skills; all of which have been reasons for recent reconsideration of death penalty cases. Often, a conviction can boil down to something as simple as the fact that the defense can never match the funds that the State can produce for research or investigation in a case of life and death.

Some jurisdictions however, having been forced through scientific testing to release death row inmates, have placed a moratorium on all death penalty prosecutions, until they can work out the kinks in the system. It will never happen. But can you imagine being on death row for 15 years because someone identified you at trial? The DNA testing shows you could not have been the one who committed the crime. So they release you back to the streets. They never caught the real criminal. They never investigated the torture that made you confess to the crime. They never examined the process to determine how you were misidentified in the first place. And they never prepared you for the 21st century while you lost half of your life to the prison system. You come out of the jail and the first thing you are asked is, "Are you angry?" All these people can really say is, "I've been telling you for 20 years that I didn't do it. I'm just glad someone finally listened before they stuck me with that needle."

Unfortunately, it's not enough to listen. In America, you have to do something in order for the system to work. Mumia Abu Jamal's case galvanized people around the world to consider the issue of the death penalty. The world was watching because white/privileged voices took up his cause and began to assert public pressure on the issue of the death penalty. However, because the death penalty disproportionately impacts on minorities, do not expect that level of support to continue. The death penalty proponents have taken the "DC Sniper Case" and Osama Bin Laden and will use fear as a poster for the need to deter. No one will ever be willing to raise a public voice in favor of either of these cases, no matter what the issue is or represents. What therefore is being deterred is debate. Thus, they are assuring that the system never gets the proper scrutiny it deserves.

Proper scrutiny simply means the voice of the people. The voice that I keep reading and hearing about that is supposed to be the most powerful since the civil rights/anti-war movement of the '60s is "Hip-Hop." YOUR GENERATION. But your generation is caught up in its image. "Hard." "Thug Lovin." "Jiggas." And all it is, is IMAGE. All form, no substance, you stand for nothing. In your effort to "get paid," you are selling your image to Wall Street. Rich white males who invest in the exploitation of poor people's plight and images in music, cinema, sports, and criminal justice. Your lyrics, your speech, your style, your attitude is moving a generation of kids who see you as Rocky Sullivan, heroes, because they have no other heroes to move them. Young girls want to be Beyoncé, Janet, Britney, Christina. If Madonna looks like a "hoochie," if Mary J is a "ride or die chick," it's "chill." It's an image that Wall Street is selling young girls as "hot," "sexy," "real" and therefore, powerful (and, if not worthy of respect, it's at least relevant). So these young followers show up to the Puerto Rican Day parade looking like J. Lo, Ashanti, Eve, or Lil' Kim, with their breasts and backside all out. Some bro, on the other hand, with LL's or Jay Z's lyrics on his mind wants to live "la vida loca." After all, he's got a 40 oz. in him (why not, Dre is down with it) and he's looking at the girlies thinking, "Shake that ass, show me what you're working with." He's a "wangster" or a "thug," and therefore, he believes, entitled, because that's what comes with the image. After the riot, the collision of these images causes, everyone goes home feeling disrespected. I wouldn't give "50 Cent" fifty cents for the images this generation is riding to fortune and fame.

Does any of this sound like an image to be respected? Where do your values come from and where are they leading you? Isn't it obvious? Your images aren't just marketed to sell products. Your images are selling a public perception that is manifesting itself in young boys who value nothing but the dollar (the Bling) or their own personal pain or passion. Society takes these images, sees him in the courtroom, and votes guilty to perception before they ever hear a fact in his case. One prosecutor in a recent case argued to the jury referencing a young black male who testified for his friend, "If you saw him on the street would you trust him?" He might as well have said the same thing they said in the racist movie that sparked the rise of the Ku Klux Klan in the early 1900s, Birth of a Nation... "The Niggers are coming."

I often talk with Larry about the day he confronted armed police literally scaring me into lunacy. Today, I understand one thing about that incident. It is something that Patrick Henry understood when he said, "Give me liberty, or give me death." It was understood by Malik El Shabazz (Malcolm X) who said, "The price of freedom is death." Even a man with nothing deserves to be respected and when he is not respected, he sometimes is willing to fight for what he sees as respect, die for this respect and, unfortunately, at times, kill for respect.

Criminal justice is a system that will never respect you unless you demand that it does. This generation has the money, the power, the voice to change this system for the better. But unlike Rocky Sullivan, your generation has shown that it could give less than a damn about the kids that it rides like a horse. Your lack of a movement and your lack of understanding about the times you are living in is a sentence of death for the generations that follow and you thereby, are signing your own death warrant. If you don't have any respect for your own, who will? I'm sure that one day someone will step to this generation of opportunist and sellouts, feel disrespected and put an end to it. It may not be as vicious or as cold-blooded as a murder in a courthouse, but it's coming. The government is hell bent on attacking the Fourth Amendment (unreasonable searches and seizures), the Fifth Amendment (due process), the Sixth Amendment (right to counsel) and is positioning itself for its attack on the First Amendment (freedom of speech, petition, and protest), through the FCC and the Patriot Act.

The death penalty is nothing more than the absolute demonstration of the disrespect that the system has for you, young people. Nothing more, nothing less. You poor, you uneducable, you drainers of the real American, poor white trash, wetbacks, niggas. In the face of government sponsored death and destruction, you "shake that ass," or chase cyber dreams, when you know disrespect and death firsthand. You see death everyday in the dreams of your families, friends, or contemporaries. Your generation is the first in history with an international connection to one another and your solution to the destruction being visited on your world is to exploit it for personal profit (as the system does).

There are more than two million persons in prison in this country, many of whom never understood that they followed a lifestyle or found their man/womanhood in an image that is created in a lab or a boardroom. Many of whom never knew the impact that your fake images have on juries, judges, and a host of others who rock to the "Hip-Hop" beats behind closed doors, but perceive any young person accused of a crime as having no real value to society.

Rocky changed his image to save some kids. Honestly, if he were not about to die in the electric chair, he would not have sacrificed his image. The "Hip-Hop" I grew up knowing was stronger than that. It was created to save a generation. Your values must change again in order to save a generation. Change your ways "Hip-Hop" or it may be your own children's screams and cries for respect/justice that tell you, "Yo Hip-Hop. You were my hero, but you went out like a punk." Not because you wanted to, but because in the final analysis, that's all you really are.

Welcome to the Real World

"Welcome to the real world, as I ponder and wonder,
Heart clash with mind like the crash of thunder..."
—Ebony Blade

What I am telling you is the real world of criminal justice. In your mind you're thinking, it can't be that bad. In your heart, you know what I'm saying is the truth, the whole truth and nothing but the truth. Where have I heard that before? When you battle with whether to follow your heart or your mind, understand the following examples taken from recent headlines.

HEADLINE: In Los Angeles, a street crime officer was busted for stealing six pounds of cocaine out of the evidence locker. He never would have been busted, but for the fact that he signed for it. Idiot. Once busted, he confessed that he and his partners fabricated cases against innocent persons, shot innocent citizens, had witnesses to their crimes deported, lied under oath at various trials, and committed a host of other crimes including profiting off the drugs they allegedly seized.

What does that say about the real criminal justice system? It says volumes. Any cop who testifies in front of a jury that the police secure the narcotics in an evidence locker and are unable to gain access to it is probably lying or naïve. You now have an example of how easy it is for the police to convict you with a lie. You now have an example of how easy it is for the police to fabricate a case against someone. (Use drugs from an old case or not report all that was seized). You also now have a real world example of why there is a presumption of innocence in criminal cases; the government representatives lie and will lie if given the opportunity.

Before Tupac, there really was a Machiavelli, who wrote, "Power corrupts and absolute power corrupts absolutely." Whenever the sole witness in a case is the police, you should remember the real Machiavelli.

By the way, if this public servant stole the drugs with the intention of selling it or delivering it back to the streets (which is what he did), was he in possession of CDS with the intention of distributing? Sure he was. He and his partners got less jail time for the theft, the intention to distribute, the fabrication of evidence, the lying under oath, the destruction of innocent lives, and a host of other crimes (in the cases that were later exposed) than the person who was originally busted for the drugs. This cop and his partners had witnesses deported, shot civilians who witnessed their crimes and no one in the prosecutor's office noticed?

HEADLINE: How about Tulia, Texas, where one cop reigned terror on an entire community, convicting nearly 50 persons on his word and investigations alone, while arresting many more on drug charges? It was eventually exposed that he was making up the facts as he went along. It was exposed because some lawyer discovered that this public servant was somewhere else at the time he was allegedly observing the drug activity he was reporting. But where was he getting the drugs? Where was he getting the evidence to support his cases? And where was the prosecutor? They stood by, watched and supported this assault on innocent lives because the victims were black and poor.

HEADLINE: In New York, four police officers killed an unarmed man in his hallway. They fired on him 43 times according to some reports and 41 according to others. Amadou Ahmed Diallo was struck 19 times and probably died instantly. The police officers in New York had a rule whereby they did not have to speak about a shooting for 48 hours. Other jurisdictions have similar rules and it's remarkable how cops, in areas where minorities live, have these rules (e.g., Prince George's County Maryland). Some say it gives the police time to get their story together. The New York officers were indicted in the Bronx where the population is predominately minority. These shooter cops are white and not from that community. The district attorney in the Bronx is black. After being indicted by this black prosecutor, the officers faced the prospect of going to trial in the Bronx. In the Bronx, the cases are assigned to a judge who will then handle the matter from arraignment to trial. This judicial assignment is done by the luck of the draw. A black female judge won the draw. Immediately, the matter was moved for a **change of venue** and it wound up in Albany, New York. Albany is a predominately white (Eurocentric) jurisdiction and the outcome was inevitable.

In the real world, you now have an example of the disrespect that the system has for minorities. Minorities could not be trusted to judge or administer this matter fairly so it was shipped someplace where the white officers could get a "fair trial." This is why I want open-mindedness in the process. Keep your idea of fair. "Fair" is relative to someone's experiences. When you step into a courtroom, you are looking for justice. All you will find is people who have no reference point from which to judge you or to understand the conduct alleged or the people involved.

Imagine what would have happened if someone was educated enough to understand that Dred Scott was alive and well in the Diallo case. When they saw that the system was putting less effort into this prosecution than they do in a three vial drug case, someone could very easily have decided that they would send a message. "I am voting guilty, if everyone else is voting not guilty." Would a hung jury have meant that the court would have to send the matter back where it belonged, in the Bronx? After all, no one would then be able to argue that the pretrial publicity didn't "taint" the jury pool in Albany. In the Bronx, they understand police/citizen encounters differently than they do in Albany. They have a history, a frame of reference. That is what makes open-minded people more appealing than fair-minded people. If you find open-minded people in the Bronx (I'm sure there are 12 left) then you know you have fairness in the process, unless, of course, that's not what they were looking for in the first place.

HEADLINE: In the real world, the majority of the people convicted of drug offenses are black males in urban areas. Logically speaking, the concept makes no sense. Drug dealing in America is a multi-billion dollar business. These young black males are selling their drugs in slums, ghettoes, and urban areas where the unemployment rate is more than triple the national average. They are selling "crack" which is the afterbirth of powder cocaine, or dope, that they dilute to the point of making it more like shooting seltzer water. If you took every urban center and all the crack sold there in a month, it would not equal the amount of powder cocaine sold in a day or generate the type of money being generated by cocaine in this country.

So where are the high rollers? Where are the people who are supporting and benefiting from this drug epidemic? I have been to Southeast and Northeast DC; North Newark, New Jersey; the Bronx, New York; Bridgeport, Connecticut; Louisville, Kentucky; Durham, North Carolina; and many other communities that are considered high narcotics areas and can see no sign that the people who would benefit from this type of foolishness exist there. Logically, I can only conclude one thing. The drugs (the real drugs) are being sold, used, and the money being pocketed is in some community other than urban centers. I just keep waiting for someone who is benefiting from it to get locked up, and it's not happening. So I look at the system and conclude, "If you are educated, wealthy and white, you don't wind up in the system (unless of course you kill your family)." This makes me wonder, again logically, if the real drug high rollers are educated, wealthy and white.

When the federal law was passed defining penalties for drug distribution, it was passed by educated, wealthy, white men. They determined that you could get life for 50 grams or more of crack. Similarly, you would have to conspire, distribute, or possess 500 grams of cocaine to get the same sentence. Crack cannot exist without cocaine. Cocaine can exist without crack. So which drug would you logically conclude should be punished more harshly? Clearly the law is designed to target the people who are involved with it. Crack is sold by poor people, cocaine is sold by others.

What do you think about a government that can protect its borders from Cuban cigars or sugar, but cannot stop the influx of cocaine? Many of us missed the numerous stories that showed U.S. government complicity in allowing the drug epidemic to flourish. These stories documented cocaine being targeted to Los Angeles street gangs by drug cartels with U.S. government sponsors and/or participation. We missed the essence of these stories because the government and the media are made up of educated, wealthy, white men. I often look for the young black boy who has the ability to fly a kite, let alone an airplane. Or book a trip from Manhattan to Disney World without mom's help, let alone chartering ships. But this poison religiously gets into the country, and onto our streets. I have been searching for 30 years for the young Latino male who is producing and manufacturing AK-47's, 9 millimeter handguns or assault weapons, and I haven't found him yet. Neither will you. What you will find is a statute in every jurisdiction where there is a ghetto, demanding a mandatory prison term for anyone in possession of these weapons for an unlawful purpose. (Only the National Rifle Association (NRA) believes you can have assault weapons for a lawful purpose and that purpose, includes protection from the government).

The point is, in the real world other forces outside of the urban community are allowing this conduct to continue. Drugs and guns lead to violence and fear. They also lead to money. It would not be good for business to stop this activity, so do not expect drugs or gun crimes to stop. But crime is like a wild fire. You cannot control it or confine it. Expect gun crimes and drugs to begin to show up in these "other" communities not normally associated with it. Those of us in the real world say, "the chickens are coming home to roost." I couldn't even spell Columbine until recently and you can bet it will get worse before it gets better.

In the real world, young means apathetic. Young means expendable. Young means you have no say. Do not fall for this trash being sold to you about "the children are our future." This system does not care about your future. It cares about "*ITS*" future (and criminal justice exposes the lie). Imagine that the criminal justice system is the shark I told you about before. It is hungry and insatiable. You are its next meal. If you are black (or some minority who is being associated with crime by the various means of education in America) you are considered breakfast. You're an easy target because of color and perception. If you are poor, you are considered lunch. The system is just waiting around for a time when your social circumstances encourage you to make that one bad decision and it will completely swallow you up. If you are young, you are considered on the menu. Eighty-five percent of all persons in jail enter under the age of 30. Sixty-five percent of the persons in jail have less than a 10th grade education and are unemployed at the time of their arrest. These are young people issues. You resolve young people issues where young people are; in schools. So when you look at the commitment government has made to your education, which is none, remember on the opposite end of that equation is the place they have committed themselves to—prisons.

In the real world, the issue is money. Follow the money trail and you will find who is behind the issue of crime and punishment. Prison is big business. Most prisons are built in communities that allegedly have no connection with crime or a crime problem. They are being built in communities where the people need jobs. These communities are mostly rural, white, and conservative. Once you decide that jobs can be supplied through prisons, you now need a product. The product is young, black, brown, or poor white people. To secure a steady flow of product, the legislators (lawmakers) and the executives (law enforcers) have declared war on drugs. Since this declaration of war has occurred, look at the rise in the prison population. Look at the number of people who have fallen victim to this non-violent crime and who are now incarcerated. Go back and look at the legislators and the executives as the crime rates across the country begin to drop. Immediately, they begin to pass and aggressively enforce mandatory terms of imprisonment, meaning a person who is found guilty of a drug crime must stay in prison for a mandatory period of time. No early release for good behavior, no parole. The judge, who the legislator and the executive have no trust in, has no discretion and must sentence you to this mandatory jail time. The prison stays full. "Mo' money, mo' money, mo' money."

Those who provide prison services from that mostly rural community with allegedly no crime, keep their jobs. Those elected members of the government who supported this assault on poor people and people of color, get re-elected. After all, they don't have to worry about a black or Latino voting block to defeat them. The black and Latino voting population is off in another county or state, in prison. Everyone knows that education, rehabilitation, and a real job will stop street level drug dealing overnight. But no commitment will ever be made by the government to any of the three because it will cost someone his/her job and someone else's votes. (It might also cause people to have less fear of their neighbor and we can't have that). Go read your **Thirteenth Amendment to the United States Constitution**. Slavery has not been abolished, it's been renamed, slave codes, Black Codes, Jim Crow, segregation, and now the War on Drugs.

HEADLINE: Not too long ago, in the real world, the President of the United States, Bill Clinton, was impeached in Congress. Millions of taxpayers' dollars were spent by an independent prosecutor to investigate his sexual conduct. An independent prosecutor was appointed because the Justice Department (that worked for and with the President) could not be trusted to investigate the

President. Clearly that would be a conflict of interest. That means that they cannot serve both sides, two masters. However, when a police officer shoots or harms a citizen, the officer is investigated by the same police department that he works for. These investigations are almost universally conducted or managed by the police and referred to the prosecutor or district attorney who bases the majority of his prosecutions on the same police officers. Unfortunately, no one is willing to say that this is a conflict of interest. Well, it is. It is more of a conflict than the Justice Department investigating the president.

There should be a Special Prosecutor assigned to investigate allegations of police misconduct with the authority to convene a grand jury and to indict and prosecute. One additional step should be taken. If the conduct of a police officer involves violence or death of a citizen, the family of the victim (victims themselves) should be allowed to appoint who they want to represent the matter as an independent Special Prosecutor. This family appointment should have the backing of the government and be paid from the government's coffers. After all, if a police officer were to shoot my brother in my town, my tax dollars would pay for the officer's defense or pay the award won by me in a civil trial. It's like me paying the lawyer of the guy who shot my brother or the government paying me with my own money. It's absurd, but welcome to the real world.

The police pay union dues and are members of organizations like the Patrolman's Benevolent Association that will hire them an attorney if they are paid members. I have no problem with that. However, doesn't it make sense that if you have to pay out of your own savings or pocket, you may think twice about your conduct the next time you are faced with a particular scenario? Of course it does. I think twice every time I park my car in New York because once I was given a $100 parking ticket. The system recognizes money as a deterrent as well, which is why almost every offense, no matter how small, comes with some monetary fine. Make these cops have to foot the bill for allegations of illegal conduct, just like normal citizens would have to do, AND MAKE THEM STAND TRIAL, and I guarantee that they would see the world from a more peaceful, professional, and less confrontational point of view. Turn the matter over to competent professionals who are not associated with the police and I guarantee that the climate of police shootings and/or abuses will stop.

HEADLINE: In the real world, science is golden. **DNA**, whatever that is, has changed the face of crime investigation. People are now being convicted and set free on DNA evidence alone. But DNA is less of a science issue in the real world, than it is a money issue. Most defendants cannot afford an attorney, let alone scientific testing. Most defendants would love to come into court with an expert that testifies opposite of the State's hired gun. You always are hearing about these cases (called high profile) where you have dueling expert opinions. Cases are won and lost on the testimony of someone giving a so-called expert opinion. When you cannot match that opinion, you give the State a serious advantage. Over 40 persons were released from death row prior to this year because the DNA testing excluded them as the perpetrator of the crime they were about to be executed for. That's frightening. But what if one person is convicted because of DNA evidence? No witnesses, no motive, just science. That's even more frightening because he cannot afford his own DNA testing and his lawyer will never understand this scientific witchcraft; neither do juries who vote to convict.

The legislature is considering various DNA proposals. Among the considerations is a bill that would create a mandatory DNA database for various crimes. That simply means that once you are charged with a particular criminal offense, your DNA is put into this database. It will be treated like a finger print. So poor JoJo gets arrested. The law already allows the court to order the taking of your blood by force, if necessary. (I know you did not know that). They say that there is no search and seizure issue or self-incrimination issue by forcibly taking your blood or saliva. But if the crime you are charged with is related to your blood, what could be more incriminating than having your blood taken by force? After all, they couldn't get you to give a statement or confess by force. With this new DNA database there is no need to smack you around. Your DNA is your signature, your confession, forcibly taken. These legislators are using the fact that DNA has excluded certain people from certain crimes to create a system that makes DNA include people in crime. No one cares that it is still a human process that can be easily manipulated by human beings with an agenda. This is just one of the outgrowths of the most hated verdict in the history of the United States criminal justice system. OJ!

HEADLINE: Crime does not pay; except when it does. For most people, that makes no sense. But in the real world, this is how it works. One day you are sitting home watching "Kobe v. T-Mac." "Boom," your door is blasted open by a police grenade or a battering ram. You are placed under arrest. You would have let them in if they had knocked, and saved the door but, they have a no knock warrant, so why not smash up your place? Eventually you get indicted and receive your discovery. In it you find something called a "CI," confidential informant. You're thinking, "Who could that be?" During most court proceedings, the government never has to tell you who it is that is giving up information about you. In court, your lawyer argues that you have rights under the Sixth Amendment to confront your accuser. The government argues that they are not charging you with the information provided by the "CI." They are charging you with the drugs, or gun, or evidence of a crime they seized as a result of the search warrant they just executed on your home or car. What's funny about this is that all of the information in the search warrant application came from this CI. You don't even know if one really exists or if the police made this up themselves (like in Tulia, TX. or in LA) and you will never know.

Or maybe you think you can trust people who commit crimes with you. After all, you grew up together. He's your "dog," your main man. He calls your mother "mom." When it comes time for trial, he's Sammy the Bull. You know he has committed as many, if not more crimes than you ever could. Sammy admitted to 19 murders. Nineteen dead people. He walked on all of them in exchange for testifying against John Gotti. I'm still not sure if they got Gotti for 19 murders. I am sure that the jury believed this mass murderer, Sammy walked and Gotti died in prison.

These confidential informants, these unnamed sources (if they even exist) are usually your people looking to free themselves in exchange for your behind. They listen in jails while you are on the telephone, they wait and they lie to get what they want, and you can't believe they would do this to you, until they do it to you. If you get arrested with them, they are the ones telling you, "you watch my back and I'll watch yours." In the meantime, they are in a Maurice Greene sprint to the district attorney or prosecutor to cut the deal that slams you. One drug dealer I cross-examined just simply switched roles because he knew the facts and the government didn't. My client became the boss, he became the runner (I saw that same scenario in the movie "New Jack City"). He got to finish his education at a historically black college, paid for by his drug dealing, got probation consistent with being a "runner." My client is doing life, consistent with being a boss, and got a different type of education. When I interviewed the cooperator prior to trial he said, "Oh yeah X is my DOG, got nothing but love for him...but you know how that is." It is remarkable how juries believe these cooperators when they testify for the government, but will reject the same "type" of witness whenever he testifies for a defendant. It's simply because the perception from the door is that you are guilty. And you are still walking around thinking that you can win in this system. Fools and criminals. Crime doesn't pay. It charges.

I'm rambling. Bouncing from one topic to the next in an effort to demonstrate what the system is really like. I'm in the real world and it's no game. You can't win! So please don't think you can.

Crime is such a dirty word and every crime has a list of victims. No one wants to see crime become the order of the day. (Unless, of course you are an accountant stealing employees 401K plans, a Wall Street insider, or a government profiteer). If you've read anything in this book and thought it made you a better criminal, you are a fool, and you will eventually get everything you deserve from the system. Every word here is meant to show you that it is a losing game. Remember me when you get involved in the criminal process, when you can't come home, when you cry at night in prison. I'll be the one telling you, "YA HEARD." You've been asking for the truth, to "keep it real"; you have it.

As my friend and brother Illiyas (a rapper known as E-Blade) says when he's "spittin" rhymes;

"This is the cruel world we live in, take what I'm givin',
But enter at your own risk, And welcome to the Real World."

For the People

When people hear me speak about criminal justice, Hip-Hop or social issues, someone inevitably wants to know, "who the hell" I think I am to be so critical. After all, this system, they say, made me a success. It has given me a forum and a chance to be heard. I know the criticism is coming and I respond by saying that I understood right and wrong before I became a lawyer. I knew what disrespect looked like long before I ever met a judge or a jury. I am now a part of this system for one reason, so that someone with some experience in the system will call it like it really is. After all, if I don't tell you what is really going on in the courts, who will?

Once when I was in law school, I got myself in a little trouble with the dean. He had invited Supreme Court Justice Thurgood Marshall to speak to the student body. Afterwards, Thurgood committed the cardinal sin. He invited questions, and thus invited criticism. As a young attorney, Thurgood had distinguished himself in the fight for civil and equal rights and was literally an icon, the best of what Howard University had to offer. He led a network of lawyers determined to break down all barriers of racial discrimination and we, at Howard Law School, often discussed and debated the brilliance of their social/legal strategy in attacking racial prejudice in the courts. When he spoke at Howard, he was an elderly man, quite the gentleman and quite distinguished. His record spoke for itself; NAACP Chief Counsel, Brown v. Board of Education, the Little Rock 9; Solicitor General, and finally, the first black Supreme Court Justice.

Everyone, who was anyone, crowded into the auditorium to hear his address. Even though I was not a big fan, I must admit that his mere presence and my knowledge of the history that was before me, was "awesome." As I sat there and listened, I began to reflect on what his and the other civil rights lawyers had done to put me in a position to live out my dream. I was proud and reflective. But at the time, all that really registered to me was my own personal passion, my image, which I perceived as "militant." Every question asked of the Justice was one of those "look how intelligent I can sound" questions. Always, the question was descriptive, complimentary, and often downright sickening. This soap opera was finally too much for me to stand. I made my way to the microphone and when it was my turn to ask a question, I sounded something like...

"Judge, don't you think you let the movement down by joining the government and the Supreme Court? After all, you can't fight in courts anymore and every important decision you make on the Supreme Court is a five to four decision and you are always on the short end. In essence, you're a figure with no power and no authority, when you once were a champion, a giant."

His response, I thought, was more intellectual hogwash.

"Son, you will eventually learn that you help where you can and let history be the judge."

I knew from the response of the guests and the audience that the question had struck a nerve. What I didn't know is that apparently someone else had addressed a similar question with what was perceived as similar venom prior to me asking my question. I, however, was hauled head first into the dean's office. The dean, Wiley Branton, was an accomplished lawyer in his own right, having been involved in the litigation that desegregated schools in Little Rock, Arkansas in the 50s. After telling me, in his polished and most diplomatic way, that I may have disrespected one of the most important black figures of the 20th century, he asked a question that I have pondered each and every day that I have been practicing law.

"Son," he said. "What do you see yourself doing in twenty years?"

I thought for a second that maybe I should give one of those self-serving, complimentary answers, that would make me sound like the "handkerchief heads" I had just heard from during the questioning of the honorable justice. That thought only lasted a second. If I was already in trouble, I thought, I might as well give him both barrels. After all, I grew up in the "bricks" of New Jersey and ran with a group that would debate Moses, if he didn't come correct. I responded, "Dean, I'm gonna open my own office and work for the people who really need our help. And since you asked, I expect to pick up where all of you left off before you all got these jobs with a government that is the enemy of civil rights, civil liberties, and people of color; you know, your enemy and mine."

He smiled at me and extended his hand. Frankly, I was expecting him to say, "Get your hat and get out." All the case law that I had learned from Professor Herbert O. Reid, on the expulsions of students, began to race through my mind. I extended my hand to him, cautiously.

"That's what I thought you would say, son. Just remember one thing. If you're as good as I think you're going to be, you won't need to disrespect anyone else to get your point across. Serve the people and serve them well for as long as you can and if I'm still here in 20 years, come back and face the questions about your career."

I had been asked by the student newspaper to do an article on the justice's appearance at Howard and searched high and low for the other person who dared "insult" the justice. I never found him and decided I would not do the story out of respect for the man simply because he was "the man." I left law school with this moment on my mind, as if Dean Branton had personally challenged me to make my mark. I was determined to make him proud (even though for the two years that I knew him I had been determined to show him up). Eventually, I learned to understand the struggle, but it took far too much head banging before I really learned that you help the people with thought, word, deed, and sometimes, when you have earned the respect, with the power of your presence.

When I was dreaming about being a lawyer, I was very idealistic. I was going to fight the good fight, expose and end the racism in the system, help the "down trodden," stand up for the "little guy," not sell out. This stand, I felt, would earn me respect and the admiration of many. I would be the next Thurgood Marshall, Herbert O. Reid, Wiley Branton, before they settled out of court for those "cushy" jobs. These "Howard men" were legendary lawyers and they moved mountains when they were in the real struggle, in the trenches.

In February 1987, I passed the bar in New Jersey. That was my ticket to the big leagues. I immediately contacted some colleagues and arranged to rent some office space. I had little to no trial experience and needed a position that would allow me to learn where I could not hurt anyone with my inexperience. Later, I found that to be the best career decision I ever made. I can't tell you how many times I have gone to courts and watched or participated in trials with attorneys having no experience, no talent, or no concern in a criminal matter. These butchers step into courtrooms around the country everyday, with someone's life in their hands. Once, I tried an armed robbery and the co-defendant was the son of a man whom I had grown up with. His lawyer was so unprepared to try a criminal case that it was absurd. I felt like I had to try the case for both defendants, so periodically I would make suggestions.

"That's objectionable counsel, you'd better say something. You can't let that in against your client."

"I don't want to object." He responded. "The judge is already mad at you; I don't want him mad at me too."

"You're kidding right? If you don't object, you have no record and that piece of evidence could mean the difference between an acquittal and a conviction."

"I was thinking that, but if the judge is mad, he might let it in anyway."

"Look man." I asserted, in obvious frustration. "If you don't object, I'm going to put this conversation on the record at sidebar."

His respect for the judge was evident. It manifested itself in fear. His disrespect for the client was also evident. It manifested itself in the fact that he had the nerve to take this matter to trial when he had neither the skill nor the courage to handle criminal matters. This kid's life mattered less than the paycheck he would get for the time he spent in court on the matter. His lack of respect for me was evident too. Throughout the trial, I pulled him aside to head off potentially dangerous ground he was opening. Since, I represented a client charged in the same case, I had to defend against the prosecution and the defense attorney's incompetence. He didn't object, so I did.

"Objection! That exhibit has not been..."

I was immediately cut off by the judge, who stated,

"Counselor, sit down. That exhibit has nothing to do with your client or his position in this case. What are you trying to do, try both cases?"

I asked for a sidebar and placed everything on the record. My client was acquitted. The co-defendant was convicted and sentenced to 15 years in state prison. Fortunately, the conviction was reversed on appeal and ineffective assistance of counsel was one of many reasons cited. The father (of the co-defendant) initially blamed me for not helping his son. Hopefully, he now understands.

In 1988, I took a position as Municipal Public Defender for the City of Newark, New Jersey. We handled nearly fifty cases a day in the trial court and I quickly learned how to make deals. In municipal court, seldom does a defendant go to jail, and when he or she does, it is because they have a background of committing offenses that is as long as your arm. In that court, I met what I consider to be, my very first mentor, the Honorable Alison Brown-Jones, a judge in the municipal court. Not only was she brilliant and beautiful, she was a powerful presence on the bench. She demanded and commanded respect. Further, she did something for me that no one had before; she critiqued and corrected. I tried numerous cases before her and always she would render a strong, concise decision. When court was over, she would call me to the sidebar and discuss the various cases that we had tried that day.

"Why did you allow this piece of evidence in?"

"What were you hoping to get out of that series of questions?"

"Your strengths are, you think quickly on your feet, but your weaknesses are this...Be sure to work on them."

"That was an excellent cross-examination of the witness, but I sensed you were backing off when you should not have."

"Do your job. Don't worry about the judge and don't ever be intimidated by a judge. You are representing a client who has put his trust in you."

Every night, I went home with some new note or some new objection or strategy that I would try the next time I had a similar fact pattern. I learned and I grew as a trial lawyer. I went in my spare time to watch trials in the federal and superior courts and would put myself in a position to bump into the defense attorneys and maybe ask a question or two. I still do.

"Counsel, why didn't you let your client testify?"

"Excuse me, counselor. I'm trying to understand why the judge ruled against you on that objection."

"Counsel, can you get the same impact of that cross if you didn't use charts or exhibits?"

"How can anyone be a drug expert?"

Some of these attorneys were brilliant and very willing to talk and educate. Most were not. My hat is off to the Alton Maddox's, William Kunstlers and Raymond Brown, Sr.'s of the world. Mr. Maddox never hesitated to answer a question no matter how irrelevant it was. He was a fierce advocate in court and, unfortunately, has been suspended from the practice of law behind his courageous stance on behalf of his client, Tawana Brawley, and the Sixth Amendment. Mr. Kunstler's war stories were always inspirational and I always needed inspiration. Mr. Brown was gracious, brilliant, and equal to the legendary reputation he has in court. I borrowed a lot of my "in court mannerisms" from his presentation. I also learned that it's not just enough to be good at what you do. You want to be twice as good, twice as prepared, and twice as sharp as the adversary, if you respect the profession. I often flashed back to Thurgood Marshall who said that as a black attorney he had to be twice as good as his white counterpart, just to be respected. I wanted so badly to be as good as these heroes, and to be respected.

As my career progressed, I began to develop a reputation as a better than average trial attorney. The reputation mattered only to the extent that it is nice to know that people think your work is good, but in this profession, I learned, you're a genius one day and a jerk the next, depending on who you ask. I always try to remain humble and go home with the intention of getting better each day. What was important to me, at one time, was to be respected, but you live and learn.

Once, I was representing a defendant in a criminal matter in a predominately white jurisdiction. The defendant, who was accused of more than 30 armed robberies, was about to go to trial on 15 counts in this particular jurisdiction. Having sent in my letter of representation, I was asked by the court to appear for the normal Monday morning calendar call. I had never been in this county court before, but I was very familiar with the demographics of the county and its reputation. When I arrived at the courthouse, I sought out the court that I was supposed to be in. It was packed in the usual manner. Everyone in the back pews was black or Latino, and everyone above the first row was white. Obviously, the back pews were for the defendants and the first row was for attorneys and court personnel. I recognized two attorneys I had met in other county courts and was pleased that they recognized and acknowledged me. I sat in the front row.

Suddenly, from out of no where I heard…

"YOU! Yeah you. Let's go, you can't sit there." This bellowing came from one of the court officers assigned to that court. His orders were addressed at me.

"Excuse me?" I responded.

"MOVE! You can't sit there. You have to sit in the back. Where's your lawyer? Are you his lawyer? (A question asked of a startled attorney sitting next to me). You should have told him he can't sit there; you can talk to him outside."

Everyone in the courtroom turned. All eyes were on me and the lawyer sitting next to me. He was white in skin tone, I wasn't.

"He's not my client." The white lawyer stated, indignantly while gathering his briefcase and hastily removing himself from any potential contact with me. I felt that I should check my deodorant or the bottom of my shoes because of the disdain he demonstrated.

"Sorry." The officer said apologetically. He then turned and addressed me again.

"Let's go. Where's your lawyer?"

Moments like these happen far more often than I care to admit. (I've been identified at least four times as the perpetrator in trials and I can't tell you how many times I've been stopped as someone suspicious in various neighborhoods while investigating a case). I have had to learn how to adapt, but this particular time it had become personal; a matter of respect. I stood and spoke.

"Let's see officer. Isn't there a sign right here that says 'ATTORNEYS IN THE FRONT ROW'? And aren't all of these men and women in this row attorneys? And did you ask any of them to move to the back of the bus; excuse me, I mean to the back of the room? Also, since I'm on a roll, this gentleman has a briefcase, a suit and tie, and so do I. Does that tell you something that maybe you and HE should come to grips with? Like maybe the Nigga might be a lawyer too, huh? And just between us, who the hell do you think you are raising your voice at?"

The courtroom erupted. People in the back pews began to applaud and give each other high fives. The eruption came just as the judge was about to take the bench. He hesitated, fearing some type of outburst. When things calmed down, the judge asked what was going on. Again, all eyes turned to me. I thought quickly and I wondered, how would Raymond Brown, Sr. handle this. In a word, dignified. I took the opportunity to address the Court.

"Good Morning, Your Honor. Muhammad Bashir, appearing for

defendant X. My apologies for the disturbance. Your officer and I were discussing the seating here and I may have said something that he mistook as insulting. However, I believe we have straightened it out with the help and intelligence of counsel here to my left. I believe we are now able to proceed without further disturbance."

When I left the court that day, the court officer apologized for the misunderstanding. The attorney did not. I picked up four clients in the court that day, two of his. As I drove home, I couldn't shake the uneasiness in my stomach and although I felt like I handled it well and with dignity, I still felt disrespected.

Back at Public Defender's office, there had been rumblings about my tactics in court. A directive had come down from the Presiding Judge that we were not moving cases quickly enough. He was right. As I began to get better at the job, I realized that many of these petty drug, drunk driving, and traffic matters could be beaten at a trial and I began to refuse the deals offered (with the permission of the client). After all, I reasoned, if they were to lose at trial, they were going to get the same penalty as if they had pled guilty, so the decision seemed to me to be obvious, take the shot at trial. After going toe to toe with a number of judges for going to trial with too many cases, I was again hauled in front of the "dean." This time it was the presiding judge.

"Son, I hear that you are very good at this job, but what you have to realize is that your tactics are holding up the court process."

"Sorry about that judge, but a lot of these cases are weak and shouldn't even be in the court."

"I understand that, but you have to realize that we are public servants and part of that position is to accommodate everyone in the system. You are hurting the system, and losing credibility with the judges."

"Judge, honestly, I don't care about the judges. I don't represent any of them."

"Well, you should change your attitude. This job would be much easier for everyone, if you were more accommodating."

"Are you asking me to plead out cases I can win, in the name of public service? Well, if you are, forget it."

This was a defining moment for me as an attorney. I took this stand on principle (not to mention how angered I was by the arrogance it took to even complain that the calendar was being held up). I knew, that by taking this stance, my days in Newark were numbered, and in less than a month, I received my notice. Initially, it bothered me. None of these complaining judges really cared about anything but getting out of court and back to their offices by 5:00 p.m. They were doing a job. I felt like I was the only real public servant in the whole system. Intellectuals, like our judges, think that you do what you can to accommodate. Soldiers fight till they die. I didn't want to be either.

Somewhere in the struggle there has to be a middle ground. Someone who understands that a defendant who gives up his driver's license because of a mistake of judgment may also lose his job. He wants someone to fight for his livelihood and his family's security. Someone must be in the system who believes that it's better to make the State prove the case rather than concede because the defendant has that right. I learned that whether a defendant faces probation or jail, the minute you compromise one right that you have, you compromise all the rights that you have. Again, that feeling was in my stomach. Disrespect. I contacted Judge Jones to see if she agreed with the assessment that I was losing credibility with the judges. She again, was strong, and more interested in educating me than debating the merits of my termination.

"The position you took, do you believe you were right?"

"Yes."

"Then live with it. Maybe it's time for you to move on to bigger and better things. Put it behind you and get to work."

I left that office with no regrets. However, I resigned in my mind that I would never take a position that would allow another "accommodationist" to decide how, where, or when I worked. Often, I would sit at home in the evenings and wonder what it must have been like for the Thurgood Marshalls of the world who felt that they were doing the right thing and that no one was willing to see or move past the norm. I rehearsed all the appropriate lines of self-motivation.

"If you are going to make changes, you have to do it from within."

"Power concedes nothing without a demand…"

"We declare the right to be a man, to be respected as a man… which we intend to bring about by any means necessary."

I eventually settled on my own: **"If you don't stand for something, then you stand for nothing."**

The more I worked in the system, the more I began to revert back to the ghetto boy who had grown up in the projects and who only got out by the grace of Allah. The intellectual me was wearing down and my ghetto persona and anger, was taking over. The anger from disrespect in the ghetto is consuming, sometimes overwhelming and often volatile.

You see the world you live in as less and when your eyes are opened, you wonder why. Why is my school less? Why does my neighborhood have less? Why are my people treated as less? Why is my word less credible? Why is my position less important? Why is my pain less painful, my love less loving? Why? Unfortunately, for us ghetto boys, there are no answers to the constant disrespect. So you grow up hard and angry and you never really understand why.

While I worked for the Public Defender, I was also representing an adjacent city, as Special Counsel handling Civil Litigation. On one rainy day, I was driving in the city, taking my children to the baby sitter. As I approached the corner, I could see a group of kids milling around. I watched, as I made the turn, and could see that a group of maybe five to seven 13 or 14-year-olds were ganging up on one little 13-year-old girl. She was "doing work," but because she was outnumbered, she was beginning to take a beat down. I stopped the car and jumped out, making sure I locked the car doors. In the car, I left my then 5-year-old son and my 3-year-old daughter. I immediately burst through the crowd and grabbed the little girl. I covered her, held her, and demanded that the others go about their business. They laughed and she cried. She was strong for a little girl, but eventually I was able to control her.

"I'm not letting you go, so calm down."

"Let me go. Let me go."

"When they get out of sight, I'll let you go. But hon, that's a fight you can't win. Be smart. Go home, call your mom or catch them one at a time, if you still want to fight."

She continued to struggle and yell, "LET ME GO." I continued to talk to her (in a driving rain) while waiting for the others to get out of sight. From out of nowhere, a police unit pulled up and the officer driving jumped out of the car.

"Let her go!" He ordered.

"What? Did someone call you or something?"

"I said, LET HER GO!"

"NO! For all you know this is my daughter or I may be saving her life. And here you come trying to play tough. Find out the facts before you start making demands."

True to what I now believe is the "police nature" my retort was perceived as confrontational and he did what all gun carrying persons do. He pulled his gun. At that moment, I could hear my son screaming so loudly that he frightened me more than the gun. I looked back at my car. He was in the back window yelling and crying,

"PLEASE DON'T KILL MY DADDY!!!!"

I was one of the attorneys representing the city this cop worked for. I was dressed for court (shirt, tie, suit, the whole uniform) and soaking wet. But again, my degree, my education, my position, my good intentions, nothing mattered. I let the little girl go, afraid now that my son was about to watch me die in the streets. She immediately looked up at me, not sure what to do, not sure who was helping her.

"Get going little girl." He said. She didn't move.

"Go on." I whispered.

She broke and ran toward the people that I had just rescued her from. The officer holstered his gun, got back in his car and drove off without a word. My son still cried. It took all day to calm him down. Finally, when he was calm, I went to the police precinct looking for that cop. I was assured that he would be dealt with, but nothing in life mattered at that time. I just wanted him, one-on-one. Angry, determined, disrespected. Since that moment, I have kept the feeling in my stomach. I have discarded all the intellectual pretentiousness that comes with this profession. The ghetto boy in me has surfaced with a vengeance. The biggest lesson I have had to learn in this profession is how to mesh my legitimate anger with my ability in court and to keep that anger from becoming frustration. I have been called "fiery/emotional" in court, so that no one has to call me calculated. "Aggressive," so that no one recognizes me as prepared. "Slick," "articulate," and "charming," to keep from admitting that I just might also be intelligent. One judge once told me that, I am "the criminal that got away." That was the only moment in his court that I ever felt respected and he was trying to insult me.

I have, since then, lectured on any number of topics and I often mention my encounter with the little girl in the rain. When I think about that incident, I still feel my anger, fear, and hear my son's cries and screams. I cry when I think about it too long. My son is now 19-years-old.

I was able to help that little girl that day in another way. She caught up with that group. This time, when they fought, she didn't have anyone to pull them off her. She took a serious beat down. One of the young girls who participated in the beat down pulled a razor and slashed the little girl's face. She received 27 stitches. I was able to identify four of the people involved in the fight, a fight that may never have happened, but for the arrogance of that police officer. The mother of the little 14-year-old "slasher" heard that I was a good lawyer and wanted me to represent her daughter. She turned out to be an old friend, so it broke my heart to have to tell her "no, I can't help you," when all I ever really wanted to do in this profession was to help.

Justice Marshall's, and his colleagues', efforts were incredible.

I've learned that when they won, I won. When they lost, I won from the sheer magnitude of their presence and the dynamics of the experiences they left behind. Both Dean Branton and Justice Marshall have passed on, and it's been 20 years, since I left Howard University. I've learned that history will judge my efforts too, not idealism, not youthful militancy, or arrogance. I am now knee deep into the struggle for justice in America and it's my choice on how I will battle. This criminal justice thing, this lawyer thing is a profession with one goal; get paid. I have to be about more than that. Everyone who understands the legacy of the struggles of the people who came before them in their various professions or vocations, must be about more than just getting paid. This is why I am so hard on judges, cops, lawyers, and "Hip-Hop."

I now know that the Dean Brantons of the world gave me that attitude. That Justice Marshall's legacy gave me the courage to believe that I could walk with giants. They remind me to look inside for respect and when you have it, use it and your abilities to light the way to justice, not for yourself, but for the people. Dean Branton, Justice Marshall and a host of others did not "sell out" like I imagined when I was young and foolish. They simply opened the way for the people like me, to see, to learn, to follow, to struggle, and eventually, to win.

I have gone through that stage of faith whereby I despise the injustices of this system in my heart. I am now in the position to speak out against it. The day is coming, I pray, when I will change it by my own hands. So "it's on." I speak out, I challenge, I criticize, and I "do work," because if I don't, who will? And I choose to start with YOU. Not because I settled out of court, but because I have to battle where the struggle is. It doesn't matter if the struggle is on the Supreme Court or in a court; at Howard University or at Little Rock, Arkansas. It doesn't matter if the struggle is in the boardroom or in the lyrics of a "Nelly" rap or in the images propounded by an Eminem video. I'm in it to win it. We all stand on the shoulders of those who came before us, opening the door for us. If we disrespect their legacy, the history, the struggle, we lose. The result of a loss in the new millennium is 2,000,000 persons in prison, the suspension of civil liberties, the destruction of the Constitution, and the entrenchment in the culture of the perception that young, black male equals criminal. To win means simply that we developed a healthy respect for the past and for the people, and we recognize that the struggle continues. It means that if you, "are not a part of the solution, then you are part of the problem," no matter how many rich idiots we produce. History, experience, struggle, and my mentors taught me that.

And gentlemen, I apologize for ever disrespecting you.

ABOUT THE AUTHOR

MUHAMMAD IBN BASHIR is an attorney licensed to practice law in the State of New Jersey. He was born in the City of Elizabeth, New Jersey. He graduated from Howard University School of Communications and completed his education at Howard University School of Law.

He specializes in criminal and constitutional law and has been a sole practitioner for 17 years. During this time, he has also represented clients in Connecticut, New York, Maryland, Virginia, Washington, D.C., and Kentucky. He has served as a Public Defender and was co-counsel in the defense of the infamous "*World Trade Center Bombing*" trial. As a criminal trial attorney, he maintains a reputation of a relentless cross-examiner and a tenacious advocate.

He is a motivational lecturer, having lectured to high school and college audiences on criminal justice and procedure. Further, he is a dedicated community servant and is involved in many community-based projects impacting on the lives of the community's youth. He also serves as Director of Policy & Planning at Image Makers Public Relations, Inc.

Married, and a father of five children, he currently resides in Maryland.

Raw Law Order Form

Use this convenient order form to order additional copies of

Raw Law

Please Print:

Name____________________________________

Address__________________________________

City____________________ **State**____________

Zip______________

Phone (   )____________________

_____ copies of book @ $14.99 each $ ________

Postage and handling @ $3.00 per book $ ________

NJ residents add 6% tax $ ________

Total amount enclosed $ ________

Make checks or money orders payable to:
The Vandy Publishing Company

Send to: The Vandy Publishing Company
112 Oak Street
Newark, New Jersey 07106